A WOF DIFFEF

THE BiG GREEN POETRY MACHINE

Cycle, Recycle, Recycle! Love the world you live in. Be good to your planet. Don't be mean, be green! Recycle! Love the world you live in...

Voices Of The Future

Edited by Helen Davies

First published in Great Britain in 2009 by:

 Young**Writers**

Young Writers
Remus House
Coltsfoot Drive
Peterborough
PE2 9JX
Telephone: 01733 890066
Website: www.youngwriters.co.uk

Foreword

Young Writers' A World of Difference is a showcase for our nation's most brilliant young poets to share their thoughts, hopes and fears for the planet they call home.

Young Writers was established in 1990 to nurture creativity in our children and young adults, to give them an interest in poetry and an outlet to express themselves. Seeing their work in print will encourage them to keep writing as they grow, and become our poets of tomorrow.

Selecting the poems has been challenging and immensely rewarding. The effort and imagination invested by these young writers makes their poems a pleasure to enjoy reading time and time again.

Contents

Whiteheath Education Centre, Rowley Regis

Whitton School, Twickenham

The Poems

Stop Pollution

Pollution what a terrible thing,
Pollution makes the world sing.
For a solution to stop pollution,
Pollution needs to be minimised,
The people around the world should open their eyes.
Don't wait for it to get worse,
The ozone is about to burst.

Jacqueline Olaifa (13)

Telford - What Can I See?

Look all around
What do you see?
I see a little play area
A football pitch
And some dull flowers.
10 years later,
What do I see?
I see children playing
Having fun,
Enjoying themselves,
I see football clubs,
Playing on proper pitches,
I see a lot of flowers,
Bright and beautiful.
I can see families having fun,
I can see less crime,
Yes I can.
I believe the children are our future,
Good education
And opportunity
That's what I believe.
What I can see,
Might not be what you can see.

Naomi Jenks (14)
Abraham Darby Academy, Madeley

1

Wouldn't It Be Great?

Wouldn't it be great if we lived in a better place?
A place of lush, green grass
Shiny new parks
Colourful flowers
A place to go, a place to relax . . .

Wouldn't it be great if we lived not in fear?
No litter
No stabbings
No fights
But neighbourly love, a wave and a 'hello' when passing in the street . . .

Wouldn't it be great if we lived in an educated area?
Extra curricular activities for all
Team work
Taking part
Fun learning
Schools that children wake up and want to go to . . .

Wouldn't it be great if we lived in a friendly place?
People who help you when you stumble
People who greet you with a genuine smile
People who care and love
Not for money, not for anything, but for you . . .

Wouldn't it be great to say:
'I come from Telford!'

Gemma Polatajko (15)
Abraham Darby Academy, Madeley

Environment

What is the matter with the environment?
All the council sitting,
Making silly notes,
Telford parks are a real dump,
Littered full with drugs and drunks.

There's no real place for us to go,
And you wonder why we walk the streets,
Give us somewhere we can go and chat,
Play pool, have fun and have a real good laugh,
These are some things we really need,
Only basic needs!

Build a hall we can hang at,
Keep us out of trouble at night,
Clean the parks,
Make them safe,
A haven for us to go,
So we have no need to walk the streets.

Kelly Turner (15)
Abraham Darby Academy, Madeley

What I Would Change About Telford

T he teenagers need somewhere to socialise, let's build them a surprise.
E lderly people need to be respected, instead of sometimes being neglected.
L ife in Telford is becoming bleak, it needs something to lift people's feet.
F orests and greenery is becoming scarce, while,
O ffices and buildings stretch over a mile.
R oads are running right through the town, now there are more cameras
    hanging around.
D o you remember the times when none of this was true?

Zoe Ayton (14)
Abraham Darby Academy, Madeley

3

A Lovely Grim Place

I walk down the street
With only my thoughts
Whistling a soft tune
To the sound of my feet.

This seems such a nice place
But why am I not happy?
I look around but all I see is destruction
Getting worse and worse.

Rubbish surrounds me,
Closing in on me, from every direction,
Destroying the lovely surroundings,
How could anyone do this?

To my left there is a deserted park,
Once there was a lovely place,
But now, it has been vandalised,
Broken and grim.

Libby Skinner (14)
Abraham Darby Academy, Madeley

Baa Baa Black Sheep Has No Wool

Baa, baa black sheep, have you any wool?
No sir, no sir, no bags full.
Why is it that you have no wool?
I have no home, no green grass to eat till I'm full.
How can we help, oh wise black sheep?
Bring back green fields, give us sheep somewhere to sleep!
Somewhere for kids to roam free and unbound,
Somewhere untouched by bricks, cement and the pound, pound, pound.
Of workers building a grey paradise,
A concrete jungle, home of rats and lice.

Dominic Brady (15)
Abraham Darby Academy, Madeley

Telford

T is for Telford, the area I live in.
E is for enthusiasm; the feeling I get while walking with pride in the Telford's major woods.
L is for let-down, how I get after imagining Telford's greenery polluted.
F is for failure, how couldn't I survive without Telford's spectacular land. Fail!
O is for outstanding, environment; no pollution. Outstanding!
R is for rivers in Telford, the clear, transparent trickle on a Sunday morning.
D is for the detention I get while, daydreaming, me out in the wild, beautiful and free.

These are the reasons I wake up in the morning,
Open my curtains with enjoyment,
And gleam with hope,
As I gaze up into
Telford!

Aston Welch (14)
Abraham Darby Academy, Madeley

Telford Poem

Telford, it's got lots to do, places 'to be'
But it's not being looked after by its people you see.

There's litter on the ground, fights on the bus
Under-aged drinking, you wonder why there's such a fuss.

It needs to be changed, right here, right now,
It's you and me that need to do it and I'll tell you how.

Think before your acting takes place,
And when you're doing 'wrong' wipe that grin off your face.

We need to appreciate Telford for the things it's got,
The town centre, the cinema, the parks, yes, that lot.

Do your bit to make Telford a place that's fun, friendly and clean,
If we make it nice we may get another visit from the queen!

Helen Davison (15)
Abraham Darby Academy, Madeley

Animal Extinction

You can be a cow
Eating grass
Until you have a good mass
Be a rabbit
That hops and hops
Until he gets to the hole.
You can be a bird
That flies and flies
Up in the sky.
Or a frog
That goes puddle to puddle
Until he finds a muddle.
But you'll never be a . . .
White tiger
Hiding in the snow
You'll never be a panda
Eating bamboo in China
You'll miss lots of animals
If you keep killing them.

Irene Gomez-Vera (14)
American School of Las Palmas, Spain

Global Warming

I like the Earth
I like the blue sea,
I like the blue sky,
And I like the blue lagoon,
And I don't want these things to die.

I like the red apples,
I like the red strawberries
And I like the red noses
But because of global warming
There will be no more noses.

I like the white snow
I like the white clouds
And like the white cotton
But maybe the snow will go
All these wonderful things that the Earth has
Will become trash
If we don't stop global warming.

Lucas Tomas Kolakovic (14)
American School of Las Palmas, Spain

Global Warming

The world is suffering
Suffering from global warming,
With all the trash buffering,
And its ice melting.

The ozone layer is almost finished,
And the ultraviolet rays are entering.
All the ice has vanished,
And the sea tide is increasing.

Carbon dioxide is in the atmosphere,
But being absorbed by plants,
And pollution is already here,
With the oxygen on the plants.

Cars, trucks, aeroplanes and helicopters,
All exhaling CO_2,
And the sun is with the farmers,
Creating O_2.

Suraj Rajani (14)
American School of Las Palmas, Spain

The Planet Earth

P lease save the Earth.
L ove your planet.
A nd it will love you.
N ow we must act. *Now*
E mpty the planet of rubbish.
T ry not to spoil it.

E arth is dying.
A death.
R ecycle.
T ry to keep the Earth alive.
H elp us to save it. *Now.*

Liam Ross (14)
Barbara Priestman School, Sunderland

Saving The Earth

P lease stop power plants
O ur Earth is getting killed
W e must stop power plants
E arth is in danger
R ecycling saves our Earth

P ollution is killing our Earth
L ight pollution is wasting electricity
A cid rain is killing plants
N oise pollution affects our health
T he pollution is killing people and animals
S top this *now!*

Andrew Robins (13)
Barbara Priestman School, Sunderland

Planet Earth

P lanet Earth is where we are.
L iving here is good.
A nd we want to save it.
N uclear weapons are dangerous.
E veryone is trying to save.
T ry not to spoil it.

E arth is our planet.
A nd we are killing it.
R ecycling will do it good.
T ransport can be bad.
H elp us to save it. *Now.*

Nathan Defty (14)
Barbara Priestman School, Sunderland

Eco Friendly

G reen is more friendly
R ubbish there is no need.
E arth is our home and where we feed.
E arth has looked after us so why don't we look after her?
N ow all we need to do is look after you.

I 'm sorry for this Miss Mother Earth.
S o what can I do to help you?
S illy, just recycle
U se your bicycle instead of a car.
E co is one
S o clean up, recycle, switch the lights off, walk instead of driving . . .

Kenneth Laverick (14)
Barbara Priestman School, Sunderland

Things About Environments

E nvironments are sometimes nice.
N ever always nice.
V ery hot!
I t's getting hotter by the day.
R eal problems for the Earth.
O ceans rising by the year.
N o more CO_2 emissions.
M urdering the plants.
E verything to stop this killing the Earth.
N o more pollution.
T he things of day to day life of Earth.

John Kenny (13)
Barbara Priestman School, Sunderland

Environment

E vil in the world we must wash away
N ever litter in the parks and streets
V ery nice to recycle
I gnorant people are smoking
R ide the circle of life
O ffensive are cars that harm the ozone
N ice people always bin their rubbish
M ucky rivers are dying because of litter
E vil is running away
N aughty people do not listen to clean words
T ell all to pick up a bottle and bin it.

Anthony Lock (14)
Barbara Priestman School, Sunderland

Save The Environment

We should stop cutting the trees
And stop with all the factories
Stop with all the cars
Or we might crash into Mars
Try to use less energy
Or we start to be the enemy
We should try to recycle
Or try and use our cycle
Try to use less fumes
Or the Earth might go *boom!*

Jordan Hackles (14)
Barbara Priestman School, Sunderland

The World

T he trees are getting cut down.
H ills have snow on them but we cause acid rain.
E arth is becoming extinct.

W orld is getting destroyed.
O ceans are flooded.
R ivers are flooding, affecting people and animals.
L ions are becoming extinct.
D isaster all over the world.

Michael Moon (14)
Barbara Priestman School, Sunderland

The World

T rees are being cut down.
H ouses are taking over.
E arth is being destroyed.

W ater is being wasted.
O ur cars are causing pollution.
R ivers are flooding.
L ights are using too much energy.
D o your best to save the world.

Ryan Tennant (13)
Barbara Priestman School, Sunderland

For A Happy Green World

Please recycle, go green
Maybe turn off the tap
Ride your bike to school

Never forget to
Tell your school not to waste water
Do it for all people.

Laura Fearn (14)
Barbara Priestman School, Sunderland

Saving The Rainforest

We need the rainforests,
Animals need them to live.
If the rainforests go,
All the animals will die from starvation.
So the rainforests must stay.
Stop the deforestation.

Emily Lavan (13)
Barbara Priestman School, Sunderland

The World

Look at the world
Look at all the beautiful things
The flowers, the trees, the oceans,
The animals, the forest, the rivers
The wonderful things it gives to us.
Everything is green.

Then litter, extinction, war, racism,
Pollution, climate change, poverty.
They all came into the world.
The world was turning brown
It's all the cars' and factories' fault
People would say.

But what they don't realise
Is that it is their own fault
They drop litter, kill animals,
Kill people, abuse people.

Everything should stop
It's going far too long
If only people can help
To make this world a better place
So everything can go back
To being lovely and green.

Olivia John (12)
Bishop Stopford's School, Enfield

13

It's Time To Change

(An extract)

This time I'm going to make it different
Because I'm fed up of feeling like a victim
I'm fed up of boys being caught dead by a knife
Because they're living the wrong kind of life
Now we're all stuck in this squashed position
Because the world's feeling all the symptoms
Of God with a broken heart.
Does that really make us *smart?*

I could kill you if I wanted to
But that would make me like you
You ask why I'm so angry
Well maybe because you're hurting me!
I'm fed up of runaways leaving as young as seven years old
You're not destroying my body but killing my soul
They're sleeping in the back seat
They're full of rage and their flesh is weak.

Growing up in this kind of world I don't get a chance to dream
I'm fifteen and already know the names of dirty magazines
There were wars going on that I barely knew
Didn't know people were dying as young as two.
I see my friends getting abused and I can't fake it
Creepy men downloading pictures of children naked
What type of demons are in these men's minds?
That they still can't escape from it and end up doing time?

After prayer meeting I see you getting high
You want to be accepted so bad you're willing to die!
Even tried to tell you but you weren't brave enough to see
Your low esteem and insecurities.
Can't you see I'm on my knees, can't you hear me crying?
I can't take this load anymore; I'm fed up of trying!
It was no lie, *you reap back what you sow*
Like everything you do, it is really hard to let it go?

Mary Akinsulire (15)
Bishop Stopford's School, Enfield

14

Let's Keep It Green

The Earth is getting warmer day by day
Icebergs melting, water levels rising,
Floats and landslides causing destruction,
People are suffering, sealife dying.
All these things happening.
Let's keep it green.

Cars, buses, trains and planes,
Travelling each day to school and work
Carbon emissions polluting the air
Why not try cycling or walking today?
Let's keep it green.

We know we should recycle,
But still we don't.
We throw everything away and buy more stuff.
Filling up the Earth and using up resources.
Stop being litterbugs and
Let's keep it green.

TVs, radios, phones and computers
These are all polluters.
We take these things for granted.
Leaving them on standby.
We need to switch them off.
We need to try.
Let's keep it green.

Ashley Fagan (13)
Bishop Stopford's School, Enfield

Would You Rather?

Would you rather live in a world with toxic waste water,
Or would you rather live in a world with fresh water?
Would you rather live in a world with acid rain,
Or would you rather live in a world with fresh rain?
Why not be green and make the world gleam?

Olatunji Balogun (12)
Bishop Stopford's School, Enfield

15

Save The World

Give a little effort,
Get lots more in return,
Make a wise decision,
Help the whole world learn!

Use time to grow a garden,
Or maybe plant a tree,
Help make the air less toxic,
For kids like you and me!

A century of changes,
Why not make one together?
Lots of things could be avoided,
Not just a change in weather!

Every choice can make us move forward,
And likewise set us back,
But we won't go down without a fight,
Our last chance, *attack!*

It doesn't matter, old or young,
Shape or size,
Boy or girl,
We can make a difference,
Be a hero
Save the world.

Shamyia Bernard-Blackstock (13)
Bishop Stopford's School, Enfield

Keep Earth Green

Does anybody care
That we're killing the
Environment, Earth and humanity?
By the time we're finished
There will be nothing!

Does anybody care
About the animals and the environment Earth?
About the animals being killed and dying?
About the animals which have no food?
Does anybody care?

Does anybody care
That when the sun rises and sets
People are dying of hunger and thirst?
And the people who beg for water
The people who starve?
Does anybody care?

Does anybody care
About the world we are killing?
The ground we stand on?
About the environment and humanity?
Does anybody care about the Earth?

Paidamoyo Mapfeka (12)
Bishop Stopford's School, Enfield

17

Save Our World

At the moment how aware are you,
With the things you say
And the things you do?

There are many things
That the environment needs,
Like less pollution
And the end of cutting down trees.

We say we understand,
And we try to do good.
Yet we still do not do
The things we should.

We jump in the Jeep
Three cars to a home,
And the whole world over
Populated with mobile phones.

So don't complain
When the roof comes tumbling in,
You should have stayed home,
And recycled your bin.

Jaydine Richards (13)
Bishop Stopford's School, Enfield

Nature Is So Great

Nature, nature is so great
Why is it not treated at the highest rate?
Pollution here, pollution there
Pollution here and everywhere
The Earth is good
So why do we waste the wood?
So let's find a solution
To stop pollution
So let's all have a rebirth
To save the Earth.

Karyme Cuthbert
Bishop Stopford's School, Enfield

Think Of A Planet

Think of a planet without any flowers.
Think of a planet without any trees.
Think of a planet without any rivers.
No nature here, no nature there.

Think of a planet without any mammals.
Think of a planet without any fish.
Think of a planet without any bugs.
No animals to kill, so none for our meal.

Think of a planet without any fumes.
Think of a planet without any acid rain.
Think of a planet without any pollution.
More nature here, more animals there.

Think of a planet with big green plants.
Think of a planet with strong, healthy animals.
Think of a planet with lots of happy faces.

The planet is a delicate place,
Recycling will help the human race.

Leonie Mills (13)
Bishop Stopford's School, Enfield

Save The Planet

I want to save the planet and maybe you do too

I don't want to make greenhouse gases by throwing my water bottle
on the floor.

I want to make a jacket or hat by just realising how much rubbish is in
the world.

We could walk to school, or cycle to work instead of using the car.

If we just did all these little things it really could go far.

So if you've left the tap dripping at home or left the TV on standby

Think about what you've just read and start changing your life.

Hannah Buller (12)
Bishop Stopford's School, Enfield

19

The Earth Poem

The Earth,
That we pollute so much.

The Earth,
That is tender to touch.

The Earth,
That looks after me and you.

The Earth,
Which our cars drive along.

The Earth,
The planet that holds nature's song.

The Earth,
That has graffiti on the walls.

The Earth,
That creates our shopping malls.

The Earth, the Earth, the Earth.

Triston Williams (13)
Bishop Stopford's School, Enfield

Save The Plants

Save the plants
Do not say I can't
Think that they are one of you
And feed them as you should do
Love plants as you should
And I think you would.

Save the plants
Do not say I can't
If all of us work together
We can achieve more than ever
Love plants as you should
And I think you would.

Özge Yelken (13)
Bishop Stopford's School, Enfield

20

In Our One And Only World

When I see little children suffering and crying,
I think, why should they be treated like this?
Their hope for love is dying
Their life is burning out
They feel they have no reason to be happy
They need our love and hope
In our one and only world

Have you ever seen anything so wonderful
As when the trees are loved?
Out there in the horizon you know there's hope
Because we know people care
There is no place in the world
Where trees are not being hurt
In our one and only world
It may be my fantasy
But everything will be how we want it
In our one and only world.

Benita Olasoju (12)
Bishop Stopford's School, Enfield

Killing The Planet

You have light, warmth and water,
I have a cold
You leave the TV on,
I become sick,
You leave the phone plugged in,
I start to die,
You never care,
You repeat, I die,
Repeat die,
I sacrifice,
You murder me.
No help, no me
Save the planet.

Trini- Maria Katakwe (13)
Bishop Stopford's School, Enfield

A Big Step For The World

It's time that we stop global warming
So we can wake up smelling fresh air in the morning
If we don't clean this dump right now
This world will be less safe and sound

Do we know how many trees we cut a day?
We're losing oxygen but getting more pay
If we don't want the world to end soon
We need to plant trees so oxygen can flow through

Now there is no time to waste
We know what to do so let's not wait
If we start putting litter in the bin
Then we will stop living in sin

Everyone has a part to play
We rely on each other every day
As a world we work together to get things done
We make great things happen if we stand as one.

Kwakw Tandoh (13)
Bishop Stopford's School, Enfield

Why Are We Not Trying?

The world is slowly dying,
But why are we not trying?
The world is getting polluted,
But why are we not trying?

The wildlife is dying,
But why are we not trying?
The schools are letting out gas,
But why are we not trying?

Every piece of litter
Is helping the world die.
So why don't we just work together.
And just try?

Sam Watson-Price (13)
Bishop Stopford's School, Enfield

Crazy Place

The environment is a dangerous place,
Let's make it safer, without a trace.
Are you aware of the things we do?
Let's make it better for me and you!

Electricity, gas, petrol and waste,
All mixed up makes a crazy place.
Cereal, juice, pasta too,
Prices going up, what can we do?

Cardboard, paper, don't throw it away,
Save it for a rainy day.
Turn your lights off before you go to bed,
Come on you lot, you're lazy heads!

Only a slight percentage, help us out,
Let's fix that right now, without a doubt.
I hope you listened to my song,
Because you'll be singing it all day long.

Lydia Weigel (13)
Bishop Stopford's School, Enfield

Humanity And Earth

People of the world, what have we done?
We have destroyed animals and plants
And now they are gone
What are we doing?

People of the world, what have we done?
Doesn't anyone care about the world?
Do you all want to die?
There will be nothing for the world.

People of the world, what have we done?
Animals are being killed
People have no food to eat
And now we need help.

Damilola Osibeluwo (12)
Bishop Stopford's School, Enfield

23

Smoke

The world is dying slowly,
But why are we not trying?
The acid rain, why does it not go away?

But nowadays everything is smoking
The cars are letting out smoke,
The warehouses are smoking.

But we think the Earth is joking
But it is choking
Our ozone layer is breaking
A hole is peeking.

But we are not trying.

Femi Onanuga (13)
Bishop Stopford's School, Enfield

The Green Machine Poem

Some people are so selfish
Some people are so mean
When it comes to the environment
I like to think I'm green
I never waste electricity
The water or fuel
I always recycle
So trees can grow real tall
I know it's not a lot
But I always do my best
And if someone does the same
Nature will do the rest.

Yasmin Costa (13)
Bishop Stopford's School, Enfield

Imagine

Imagine a place with no fresh air,
A place where the atmosphere is openly bare,
Imagine a meadow without any flowers,
A meadow with no life or excitement.
Imagine a child having to drink rotten dirt,
Then realising that it adequately hurts,
Imagine a river full of dead animals' remains,
And then having to take a bath in it,
Without a sign of care and inaccuracy,
Imagine a place with no sign of joy,
The sorrow that's shared between the girl and the boy,
A world where air is defunct!

Mabel Osejindu (15)
Bishop Stopford's School, Enfield

The World's Ending

The world's so green
Unlike the sky
We're killing the Earth
And now could die
The cars start driving faster
With fumes coming out of their engines
The ice is melting
The world's just ending
The people in London
Running scared from the credit crunch
It's there.

George Jones (12)
Bishop Stopford's School, Enfield

We Can Make The World Green

We can make the world green
We can make the world green

Let's switch off instead of standby

Let's recycle instead of throwing away

Let's change the world together

And make the world green
We can make the world green

Green, green, green!

Dorcas Gyasi (12)
Bishop Stopford's School, Enfield

Stop

Plants are dying
What happened to the world?
Cutting trees down
What happened to the world?
Destruction, bombs, fire,
What happened to the world?
Turn it around, turn it around,
Now, now
No more plants are dying
And no more children are crying.

Rebecca Manu (15)
Bishop Stopford's School, Enfield

The World Is So Green

We can all help the environment
By recycling today, no litter, can you imagine
What the world would look like?
Probably not, because the world is full of it.

Planet Earth can be saved but
Everyone is needed to help
The Earth is crying out for help
It's just us the world needs
Can't you see the Earth is sad and so are you?

Shauna Rowe (12)
Bishop Stopford's School, Enfield

Untitled

You have to recycle
Saving paper and card
Keep the oxygen
And plants too

You have to reuse
When you go shopping
Don't get a plastic bag
Get a fabric one and use it

You have to reduce
Reduce the litter
Dropped on the floor
Save the animals that eat rubbish
And help animals.

If you don't do these things
People will suffer
People will die
So recycle, reuse, reduce.

Recycle, reuse, reduce.

Wesley Burton (11)
Earlham High School, Norwich

Environment

Environment is dying,
Africa, Bangladesh,
Loads of methane,
In the air.

Ice caps melt,
Sea level rises,
Flooding,
What can we do?

Flooding,
Heat wave,
Torrential rain
Who's to blame?

Recycle,
Reuse,
Reduce,
This is what we can do

We as a world,
Are causing climate change
Global warming.

Think, think,
Why are we doing this?

Rebecca Cunningham (13)
Earlham High School, Norwich

Litter

L itter
I s
T errible
T o
E veryone
A R ound our world and environment for the people and little children.

Kieran Lovewell (12)
Earlham High School, Norwich

Paper Or Plastic?

A
Paper bags
Compost heaps (brown bins)
Recycling plants
Bikes
Walking
Boats
Green boxes
Blue bins
These are good

B
Plastic bags
Sweet wrappers
Black bins
Polystyrene
These are all bad

What will you use A or B?
It's up to you!

Kiah Williamson (11)
Earlham High School, Norwich

Animals And Extinction

Think of all the animals dying,
Their last life is going to waste,
Our pollution is killing them,
So help our world become a better place.

When a type of animal goes extinct,
Stop and think, what if that was you?
If your mum is always using the car
Stop and do what you have to do!

Stop, and help them live!
Do a good thing for once!

Dayna Barnes (11)
Earlham High School, Norwich

The Climate's Ways

The climate's changing every day.
In so many different ways
The ice caps are melting
It will become sweltering
Recycle your materials
Like the boxes from your cereals.
In Africa the water had dropped,
So they can't grow their crops.
It's flooding in Bangladesh,
Because of our own mess.
To help them, so they don't die.
Our world could change in the blink of an eye.
We need to improve our world,
For the next generation.
Boy and girl.

Ellie Ireland (11)
Earlham High School, Norwich

The Animals

Why help climate change?
Why kill the animals?
Why when shopping should you arrange
All the bags you use?
Polar bears are fluffy,
Monkeys have got tufties.
Just be helpful.
Recycle all the things you can
Milk cartons
Paper
Cans
And bottles, are just a few to say the least.
Why not put food in the compost heap,
Or the weather will change for the worse!

Jake Brown (11)
Earlham High School, Norwich

30

Climate Change!

Well where does it really start?
It starts with us
I can tell you now the problems are everywhere
They stretch from far and wide
Even up into the sky
It's as far as starvation in Africa
Floods in Bangladesh
Oh yeah! And climate change
So you may think it's bigger than you
But you can do a lot too
Just follow three simple rules
Recycle, reuse, reduce!
And that's all you need to do!
Just follow the rules.

Katie Cooney (13)
Earlham High School, Norwich

Let's Help

If you do the three Rs you will make a difference to the world,
You will keep countries from flooding
And animals from dying.

First R is reduce
Second is reuse
And don't forget to recycle

Make a difference to the world
One is not enough
Work as a team

Stop binning, binning, binning
Start thinking, thinking, thinking.

Kye Metcalfe (11)
Earlham High School, Norwich

Problems

Plastic bags - paper bags,
Which one to use?
Paper bags are recyclable!
Plastic bags are bad for the environment, can't you see?
The 3 Rs - recycle, reuse and reduce,
The people of Africa and Bangladesh need help!
So keep those 3 words in mind,
And it's down to you to help.
Bangladesh is flooded.
Africa, overheated!
Help these countries.
Please.

Chanell Cornish (11)
Earlham High School, Norwich

We Need To Be Green

We need to be green
And make the world clean
We need to recycle
And get on our bikes
To reduce the pollution
And that's the solution
The rubbish goes into the ground
And spreads the gas around
The climate is changing and that's bad
But we don't want people suffering because it's sad
The world's in danger
But you can still help if you're a stranger.

Shahrukh Zaffar (11)
Earlham High School, Norwich

Global Warming Or Global Warning?

Landfill sites filling fast,
Environmentalists say this won't last,
Innocent children will have to suffer,
If only older people could've been tougher.
Floods, hot or cold? Who knows?
The wind doesn't care, it still blows,
Flooding in Bangladesh,
It sure is a mess.
Carrier bags, you only need one,
If not you will be filling landfill sites for fun,
Laughing, joking you may be
Just wait until you see!

Jessica Wenn (12)
Earlham High School, Norwich

Stop Racism

R   acism
A   nd
C   alling names
I   s
S   o
I M   mature.

Racism hurts people
You would not like it
If it happened to you so
Think before you speak!

Jade Hall (11)
Earlham High School, Norwich

Together!

Do you know what we've done?
Don't you realise it's not fun?
We have destroyed
We have killed.
Our one and only chance
To unite together
We can save those places in need
So come on everyone
Help us banish the mess
From such places as Bangladesh!

Kayleigh Parker (13)
Earlham High School, Norwich

Recycling

R ubbish
E verywhere
C auses
Y et more
C asualties
L iving
I n a
N ation that
G rows warmer.

Charlotte Rowe (11)
Earlham High School, Norwich

If We Don't Recycle

If we don't stop poisoning the planet
If we don't stop burning rubbish
If we don't reuse bags.
If we don't recycle
We don't stand a chance.

Nathan Tooke (11)
Earlham High School, Norwich

Recycling

R ubbish
E ven
C auses
Y et more
C haos
L iving
I n a world where
N othing is
G rowing.

Ashleigh Hensley (11)
Earlham High School, Norwich

Climate Change

Please help! There are animals dying, sea levels rising
Floods and drought, all happening because of climate change!

You can help this by:
Recycling
Reusing and
Reducing!

What we do affects everyone and everything in the world every day!
So do your bit and help save the world with us!

Jessica Walsh (12)
Earlham High School, Norwich

Africa

A n effect of global warming is
F amine in Africa because
R ising temperatures make
I t really hot so you
C an recycle or ride a bicycle
A nd you will really help.

Nathan Dolby (13)
Earlham High School, Norwich

Climate Change

Reduce, reuse, recycle
Are three important words
Either walk or cycle
To save the world

Bangladesh is flooding
Africa's too hot
They will die of starvation
Because they have no crops.

Daniel Marshall-Nichols (11)
Earlham High School, Norwich

Animal Extinction

If you live in a normal world
You will know that it's not all diamonds and pearls
So you should always know
That animal extinction you can't let go
These poor animals, it is so painful
They live in the wild and pollution is dreadful.
So please, please help us, put it right
And save these poor animals, here and tonight.

Kaya Laing (11)
Earlham High School, Norwich

Helping The World

If you are a person who recycles then you are a recycler
and you are helping the world.
Try your hardest to recycle things and stop greenhouse gases
like carbon dioxide.
Try and stop climate change, floods and ice caps melting and sea levels rising
and try and help the crops grow in other countries.
If we can do it, everyone can do it.

Kyle Picton (11)
Earlham High School, Norwich

Untitled

Please do not litter
We use this thing called recycling
If you don't recycle
You pollute the air
And climate change can help
The three Rs can help
But they can only help if you
All work together.

Jordan Dale (11)
Earlham High School, Norwich

Climate Change

Some people think that
Climate change is good for us
Because it gives us light
But in other countries they are sad
Because they're always in a flood
For they will get a disease
With this they will die in a bad state
Let's all work together!

Mheann Orias (11)
Earlham High School, Norwich

Reduce, Reuse, Recycle

Don't throw your rubbish away
Recycle it instead
This will happen if you throw it away
We will make places drier and then they will have no crops
Or it could get wetter and make places flood
Because the polar bears will drown as all of it will melt
The sea levels rise and that will cause the floods.

Frank Brown (11)
Earlham High School, Norwich

Untitled

If we work together we can stop ice caps melting
Which causes sea levels to rise which causes floods.
Really dry weather causes less crops, causes famine.
But if we can do these things to help the environment like the 3 Rs
Reuse plastic bags
Reduce the amount of waste in landfill sites
Recycle bottles, cans and more
Then it will be a better environment and stop climate change.

Alice Roberts (11)
Earlham High School, Norwich

The Green Poem

Ice caps are melting in Antarctica
People are starving in Africa
Please recycle to help these people
It's not hard, it's very simple
Buy a bag and keep it forever
It's not stupid, it's really clever
Make the sea a lot more safe
And make the Earth a better place.

Aqil Zainal (12)
Earlham High School, Norwich

Poverty

P eople have no food and drink dirty water.
O nly waiting for the rain.
V andalism happens to houses from the floods.
E veryone suffering from being too thin and having nothing to eat.
R ight now stop and help these people.
T ry and give up some clean water for these.
Y ears go by and more and more die of poverty.

Kimberley Dennis (12)
Earlham High School, Norwich

Stop Racism Now!

R espect all of us
A ll of us are the same.
C ome on people, don't be mean!
I say we are all equal
S top racism
M y mate is black and there is no problem with that.
   Make a difference today, stop racism now!

Jodie Harman (11)
Earlham High School, Norwich

My World

Pollution is getting really bad
Recycling can help, they're really sad
We're losing trees as the days go on
The smell of litter really pongs
Most African kids play in mud
In many countries they have mega floods
We can help stop pollution!

Connor Innes (11)
Earlham High School, Norwich

Racism

Racism is wrong
And yet it still goes along.
People shouldn't get treated this way,
So let's make a stop today.
This is just not fair,
So don't say you do not care!

Alisha Whitworth (11)
Earlham High School, Norwich

Recycle

Recycle! Recycle!
Use your bicycle,
For Momma Earth
If we recycle
It will save the ice caps
Reduce! Reuse! Recycle!

Samuel Quandrill (11)
Earlham High School, Norwich

Global Warming!

Recycle all your paper in the green box bin
So we can reuse it again and again.
So we can stop global warming and stop all the flooding
Together we can stop from doubling the trouble.

Kayleigh Willetts (12)
Earlham High School, Norwich

Repent

We laugh in joy
You cry in this despair
We will destroy you
My mother will punish you
But you stubborn people don't know what you did
The end is near and you'll repent

Peacefulness is what you want
But we, the people, gave it once and will never give it again
You hunt us down when we hurt you
But you think it is normal that you destroy us
You are selfish, self-centred and greedy beings
But you may have hope if you'll ask for forgiveness.

Angela Park (14)
Faith Academy, Philippines

Reminder

Whenever I eat meat
I wonder how Aunt Moo is doing
Producing delicious creamy milk
Or hung on a hook, appealing?

Whenever I don't finish my food
I wonder how children on the streets are doing
Running and skipping around, telling funny jokes
Or begging for food, starving?

Whenever I wash dishes
I wonder how Madame River is doing
Singing with her cool comforting song
Or with a weak, empty voice, drying?

Whenever I wipe my wet hand off with a tissue
I wonder how Sir Forest is doing
Standing majestically in the green clean wild
Or am I using him right this moment, filthying?

Whenever I am happy, laughing with my family
I wonder how people in war are doing
Hoping for the light of peace
Or dying and shivering with fear, hope disappearing?

Whenever I ride in a car in a traffic jam
I wonder how our guard Atmosphere is doing
Defending valiantly for our world
Or disturbed by smoky screening?

Whenever I throw trash anywhere
I wonder what's happening to our nature
Beautiful enough to run for the Miss Universe
Or rotting away, not knowing the future?

Whenever I live in peace and comfort
I wonder how Earth is doing
Living in harmony like us
Or in misery as it's dying?

Ha-Young Lee (14)
Faith Academy, Philippines

They Know

The Earth said to the tree one day,
'What is wrong with these people, I say?
They think they're doing the good for all,
Without realising they make themselves fall.'

The tree replied to the Earth down laying,
'Don't you know these human beings?
All they care about is useless things.
Out of your minerals they make jewelled rings.
What good are those for, anyway?
They can't even take them on their way
To where they came from; and when they do,
So will your minerals come back to you.'

The Earth gave a sigh; the nearest volcano
Gave a puff of smoke and a little blow
The people all around screamed and fled
As fast as their legs possibly led

The Earth spoke, in a silent deep roar.
'Do you remember, they respected us more
Than any other things their hands had made?
Their memories seem to very quickly fade.
Still, they keep records
Of extinct animals, trees and birds
What good are they? Shouldn't they thus
Preserve what is left to us?'

'True,' said the tree, oblivious to the passing time.
'If only they remember their original design.
The one they were made to be; don't you recall
What He who had made us all
He who created us, the humans and even little bees
Had made us together to be?
To serve them, yes, but don't they know
That if they destroy us, back to them it will go?
He made us to be a cycle, equal in all
Making not one out of the cycle fall
But these men: those who heap knowledge by the lump
They are the ones who mess it all up!

I guess the space between us grows
Though the promise from Him long ago
Says we are the men's; didn't he foreknow
That they'll break all the unwritten rules?

Look, look what they do!
Destroying us and our products too!
Paper? It doesn't even make a cup!
Oil? All they do is burn it up!
Land? They waste one after the other!
Their useless thing is why they bother!'

The Earth was silent, so was the tree
The setting sun was letting another shadow free
The Earth spoke silently, almost a whisper,
'Say, do you see that youngster?
He is planted next to you sound asleep
Probably tired from a good day's trip
He was planted by a young boy today
Where still with your dreams you stayed
He seemed to come here with a purpose; don't you see?
He actually cares for you and me!
Sure he is small, but when he grows
He'll tell his child all he knows
And will tell about us, how we need them
As a helper, feeder, and of course, a friend
Although they hurt us and tear us apart
We are both part of the art
We can't throw each other away
We all need each other in some way
I've noticed something; have you?
I think they know it more than we do.'

Yoo-Jin Jeong (13)
Faith Academy, Philippines

Earth

I'm an Asian
With a sensation

Who can't dare
Seeing them *tear*

The Earth
With machines,

The Earth
I imagined
From birth,

Do you believe?
It gives *you* fresh air
And *you* in return
Give air that I cannot bear

You give it gas
You give it trash
Acid rain
You give it pain

You give it . . .
Waste
Toxic canals
Polluted seas
Dying bees

Hazard
Panic
Danger
Smoke
Global warming
Terror

You give it pollution
From inside of its delusion

You hurt its animals
Like they're irresistible

You hurt its trees
Mountains
Rivers
Oceans
And high sky

44

The Earth is not a toy
That *you* play around with
You people of the Earth

You nourish it
Nurture it
Take care of it
Clean it
Polish it
Bit by bit

So do *your* part
And save the Earth
From dying.

Ye Bin Koh (13)
Faith Academy, Philippines

Extinction

This morning I found a dinosaur in my house
It looked thin, weak and scared
I wondered why it came
And wondered why it stayed
It did all sorts of reactions
It looked as if he needed a place
He ran around my house biting my sofa
So I took him in

The next day I found a white rabbit
It looked thin, weak and scared
I wonder why it came
And wondered why it stayed
It jumped around my house going in and out of the fridge
Its face was better than ever
So I took him in.

David Jeon (14)
Faith Academy, Philippines

A Cry To Become One

Momma's driving on a sunny day
And I look outside my window
A child is asking for a single coin
In his eyes I see the sorrow

I throw my garbage outside my home
These children come running at it
They desperately dig in to find food for their loved ones
And to fill their empty stomachs

I hear a yelp from a far distance
A daughter just lost her father
Unable to pay for the cure to keep him
Sadly they parted away

Now I ask myself
What has happened?
Why is the world like this?
Is it my entire fault?
What have we done?
Where has all our hope gone?
Have we given up?
Have we lost our faith?
Are we just afraid of change?
We are family
Working together
Helping each other
In becoming one

When I open my eyes in the morning
I cry just thinking about them
My heart bleeds thinking of the pain inside them
Where have our eyes and our hearts gone?

Now I ask myself
What has happened?
Why is the world like this?
Why can't we change?
Where did my faith go?
Why are we moving so slow?
Did all our love flee?
Do we just give up?
Are we going to ignore their plea?

We are family
Working together
Helping each other
In becoming one
We want our world to become one.

Gianna Llanes (14)
Faith Academy, Philippines

Be Grateful

The world is cruel for many
But even the fortunate aren't satisfied
Many of us have a home to live in
Food to eat, and a bed to sleep in
We have clothes to wear, a school to study in
And parents who love and care for us
Yet many are unhappy with what they have

Some are on the streets - homeless
Countless are starving to death because they have no food
Some are uncomfortably sleeping on hard floors
Some are wearing the same clothes they've worn for the past month
Many are envious of those who go to school
But with their insufficient funds, they are unable
Many are orphans who wander around the streets begging for money

These people are unfortunate, are living a hard life
Even a piece of wood to give them shade is like a luxurious house
Rotten food they find from trash is a grand buffet
A piece of cardboard for a pillow is a soft bed for them
A few ragged clothes are like a grand dress for the prom
A piece of chalk or rock is enough to draw and write

But those who are privileged are still discontented
We have a stable home, delicious food, a soft bed
Many clothes, a good school and parents who work hard for all of this
Think about the poor who don't have any of this
Be grateful for what you have.

Shaine Son (14)
Faith Academy, Philippines

Our Earth

We live in one world
One Earth
One planet
One land

We don't have a spare
We don't have an extra
We can't lose this one
It's the only one we've got

Can you hear it saying
'Stop giving me lung cancer'?
Can't you hear it crying
'Stop cutting my body'?

We kill what exists only here
We kill the living green
We kill the living species
We kill our own race

Can we stop this disaster?
Prevent this destruction?
Ban this calamity?
Avert this catastrophe?

Listen to the Earth
Hear the cries it makes
Pay attention to what it says
Follow its commands

Let us abolish the bad
Get rid of the pain
Eliminate the sorrow
Make agony disappear

Only possible if we work together
Only probable if we hold hands
Only achievable if we collaborate
But impossible if we don't start now.

Hajong Lee (14)
Faith Academy, Philippines

Untitled

Dear Environment

I am sorry for
hurting you and
killing you
but
thank you for
giving me everything
you have.

I am sorry for
burning you and
making you filthy
but
thank you for
sharing the clean air
you have.

I am so happy
because of you,
my friend
Environment,
because of your
sacrifice,
we the people
are living well.

Please wait for
My requital to you
I promise you that
I will save your home and
yourself by
cleaning and planting

Thank you
my friend
Environment.

Cathy Lee (14)
Faith Academy, Philippines

To Care For The People Of This World

What does the Earth see in us now?
What does it feel when looking round
when blood is seeping on its ground?
When children and women are heard screaming for mercy,
but feel the sting of bullets burning through flesh?
Smell it so horribly, guess what happens next?
What makes us who we are to hurt so many people?
What makes us kill, steal, shoot, massacre and exterminate people?
What makes us so heartless; so uncaring to let them die without even a look?
What could stir our hearts to help them?
Why do we murder for greed, power and fame?
Is it worth it to take the life of another, maybe even a mother?
We see a child cry over his mom because of a bomb.
Such are the ways of Man, but can we still change them to care for
the people of the world and work for peace to save the Earth?
It's not worth it to make such little gain, not at all! It will just make the Earth
fall into more destruction and corruption.
The healing of the Earth, the blood spilled will cleanse the Earth of its
memories to be forgotten; or may be remembered to teach those to never let it
happen again.
So that later the young will not wake up quaking in fear because of the gunfire
a-ringing just over the hill.
No birds singing. Let it not happen again, like now, but so let it be told to
remember those days and fear them still.

Steven North (14)
Faith Academy, Philippines

Every Day

More trash we have lying on the streets
More trash piling in the trash bin
One day we clean it up
The next,
Next,
Next,
It comes back again
More trash we have lying on the streets
More trash piling in the trash can
The next year we clean it up again
Next,
Next,
Next,
Every day trash lying on the street
Trash piling in the trash can
Next,

Next,

Next,
Again we clean it up
Again it comes back

What do we do this time?

Paul Jang (14)
Faith Academy, Philippines

The Past Destroyed

I remember picking flowers in the yard
But they are gone and look like lard
And the trees are gone from the woods
They are replaced by neighbourhoods
Alaska lost its beautiful and precious mountain peaks
The weather's not cold enough to get frostbite on your cheeks
The birds that chirped aren't heard anymore
And are no longer seen while they soar.

Isaiah Olsen (13)
Faith Academy, Philippines

Save Your Home

What would people think
When they see the Earth in dump?
They'd notice weird things
The ground can go bump

They'd be plastic bottles,
Papers all over the ground
There might even be soda cans
Oh wait, it's all around

Garbage, garbage everywhere
Help our world, oh please!
Plant trees, plant flowers, plant ferns, plant fungus!
Or you may never, ever see your niece

Clean your houses, clean your yards
Unplug your electronic devices
Especially vampire wires
And then you'll be known as the nicest

Save the fauna, the flora
And preserve all biomes
Save the Earth, all of you
This world is our home.

Kathleen Tan (14)
Faith Academy, Philippines

Foolish Love

'I love you, I love you, I love you
Even though you give me junk
I will conceal it for you.

I love you, I love you, I love you
Even though you give me gas exhaust
I will purify it for you.

I love you, I love you, I love you
Even though you give me stinky water
I will drink for you.

I love you, I love you, I love you
I will give you everything that I have
Because I love you'

Dying Earth said.

Daniel Choi (15)
Faith Academy, Philippines

The Recycle Cycle

I love to recycle paper
I love to be very green
So I took an old newspaper and smashed it
Creating a black quicksand pit
I mashed it some more and mixed it with water
I sighed with pride like a master potter
Then ran to find my sister's screen frame
I spread it all out and let the water drain
I waited and waited and waited
I squeezed a little, the water had faded
Then with my mum's hairdryer
Dried it like a magazine flyer
I felt so proud I showed my brother
He said, 'Next time be sure to add a flower.'

Sonya Hagberg (13)
Faith Academy, Philippines

I Hear Them Crying

I hear nature crying
The trees drying
The flowers dying

I hear the animals crying
The polar bears drowning
The birds falling

I hear the Earth crying
The trees, flowers,
Polar bears and birds . . .

I hear them crying.

Victoria Choi (14)
Faith Academy, Philippines

You & I

Green grass is what you see.
Bloody violence of World Wars is what I see.
Fresh air is what you smell.
Pollution is what I smell.
Birds and wind are what you hear.
Guns and screams are what I hear.
Water is what you feel.
Trash is what I feel.
You and your selfishness.
Me and my generosity.

Grace Jung (13)
Faith Academy, Philippines

Tick Tock

Every minute, every second
Tick-tock our world is dead
By the trash, by the oil
Tick-tock our world is gone.
Pollution here, pollution there
Tick-tock our world is lost.
Tick-tock, tick-tock,
Tick-tock, tick-tock.
Every second will kill our Earth
Tick-tock, the time is ticking.

Hanbin Yoo (14)
Faith Academy, Philippines

Homeless

A tear trickles down my miserable face
As I look around in a disturbing place
With no food to eat and no home to stay
Was that the price I had to pay?

Has the world forgotten about people like me
Or are they just waiting for us to be free?
Free from starvation and hunger we've had
Free from being abused from people who are mad.

Can't you see we're crying in pain?
But you just laugh at us and think we're insane
Can't you see we're not like you?
We don't have a home, we have feelings too.

You'll see and I'm telling you it'll be your children next
Can't you donate a penny or so?
And help us from being poor
Help us from being foodless
Help us from being homeless
Please just help us!

Umaymah Tahir (11)
Golden Hillock School, Birmingham

Beautiful Rain

Rain, rain, beautiful rain,
Why do they hate you so?
Your shimmering drip drops
Sound like a water balloon pop.

Rain, rain, beautiful rain,
Why do they hate you so?
Your colour is see-through
As it falls down from a sky that is so blue.

Rain, rain, beautiful rain,
Why do they hate you so?
You fall down low
And then create a rainbow

Rain, rain, beautiful rain,
Why do they hate you so?
I don't know,
Do you know?

Ayesha Jamil (11)
Golden Hillock School, Birmingham

The Living Earth

I gave you trees
You gave us paper
I gave you energy
You gave us waste
I gave you animals
You gave us hunters
I gave you land
You gave us landfills
I gave you the Earth
You gave us global warming.

Yasmin Bi (12)
Golden Hillock School, Birmingham

56

Why Don't You Try?

Why don't you recycle the rubbish you put in the bin?
Do something positive, refusing to recycle is a sin
You're throwing away all the world's resources
And destroying the positive forces

Let's make a change and do something good
Start to recycle in your neighbourhood
But don't leave it there
Recycle your lifestyle and start to be fair

Save water and turn down the heat
Conserve energy and get to your feet
You don't need the car when you're not going far

We need oxygen to breathe and fresh air
Leave the trees alone and show that you care
This will save all the animals crying for love
Let's make the world better, let's start from above.

Mohammed Najmul Hasan (11)
Golden Hillock School, Birmingham

The World

We live in a place
We destroy this place by
Polluting the streets with rubbish
We graffiti on the walls
We have gang fights
We never think
We need to think
We cause global warming
Why do we need cars for a ten minute
Walk down the street?
We should treat nature with respect
We never think
We never think
We need to think.

Roheel Haider (12)
Golden Hillock School, Birmingham

57

Acid Rain

Go outside in the pouring rain,
'Argh! Argh! Argh!' Scream in pain.
Can't help it, it's acid again.
Everyone in the world is going insane.
I told you not to pollute my world.
Now everything in the Earth is curled.
Can't you see the litter on the floor?
What happened to recycling, is that too much of a bore?
All your rubbish is dumped in the ground.
Next thing you know your rubbish will be all around.
Global warming is very near.
If it comes everyone will fear.
What about the animals, why are you eating them?
They're only innocent creatures, they deserve more attention.

Sadiyah Shah (11)
Golden Hillock School, Birmingham

The Earth Returns!

The Earth is ruined!
The Earth is dull!
The Earth is dirty, why don't you recycle?
The Earth is now unfriendly
People are dying for things they have not done
The people are poor, poor as can be
All we do is make rubbish
The Earth is different, as different as can be
Let's all come together and make a new Earth.

Qasif Shabbir (11)
Golden Hillock School, Birmingham

Don't Kill Your Planet!

Don't kill the Earth,
Keep it as clean as your shirt,
Don't pollute your area or country,
And make sure you don't keep the poor hungry!
Acid rain will wreck your country,
And as I said don't keep the poor hungry.
Do you think it is funny?
Don't destroy the bunnies.
The country is dirty, don't make it murky.

Hassan Sarwar (11)
Golden Hillock School, Birmingham

Our World

Look all around pollution you will see
Come help the environment you can be a good citizen for your city.
Cars and factories cause acid rain
No harm to you, but the environment takes a lot of pain!
The ozone layer is becoming very thin
Reducing pollution it can start to begin growing again.

Rose Mina Ahmed (11)
Golden Hillock School, Birmingham

Poaching!

Poaching is never fair
Two tigers are a pair.

Poaching is never fair!

They have a cub,
You're loading up your gun in the pub.

Poaching is never fair!

The cub is not very old,
And it's getting cold.

Poaching is never fair!

The father then leaves,
And the mother starts to grieve.

Poaching is never fair!

The next day you go in the forest and you see the mother and you shoot at will,
During the night all you think about is the kill.

Poaching is never fair!

Now the cub has no father or mother,
No sister or brother.

Poaching is never fair!

The cub has no milk,
Soon you will trade the coat for some silk.

Poaching is never fair!

Soon the cub will lie,
And the next minute he will die.

Poaching is never fair!

You wouldn't like your family dead,
So why go out and paint the world red?

Poaching is never fair!

Izaak Gosling (12)
Hutton CE Grammar School, Preston

The Heartbroken Animals

People aren't doing anything about it
So stop and think about them.
People giving little money
Africa, Antarctica, anywhere you want
Looking at them playing with their family
Then suddenly locked in a pen.
Bears' and orang-utans' broken hearts
Animals left to die in rotten cages and pens
It's just not right.
Whales swimming for their lives
Then caught in fishermen's nets and left to drown
Fishermen on boats and poachers on jeeps killing
For food when there is really no point.
Monkeys' and gorillas' homes chopped down
So there is nowhere for them to stay alive
Lions', cheetahs' and leopards' long grass where they hunt
Burned down so they die of starvation.
Polar bears' icebergs floating further away
So it is further to swim for them to land
So stop and think about these poor animals
No one is doing anything about it
You could be that someone
So the thinking starts now!

Michael Hampson (12)
Hutton CE Grammar School, Preston

War!

Why, why, why
Why have war?
War is terrible for those who fight it
But the man who starts it all
Doesn't fight
Didn't think of that one did you?
Ah, he just sits in his chair
And says
I declare war
Just think
What would the government say
If he had experienced war just once?
But no
He won't
But if he did he would say
Stop war
Now
And all come together and stop fighting
And if this happened
The man who starts it all
Would stop it all
Now!

Benjamin Rowland (12)
Hutton CE Grammar School, Preston

Pollution

The world is a huge polluted place
Countries spread far and wide.
People living at a hurried pace
Pollution goes into space
As pollution travels around in space
We start our cars to join the daily race
We never think of the harm it causes.
Polluted gases make it hard to breathe
The city smog is ever growing
Choking life, never stopping
Factories spewing toxic waste
This isn't good for the human race
We need to clean up the way we are
Recycle, reuse to make our planet green
We need to look at ways to power
Our cities don't need fossil power
The gases rise into the sky
Which falls to Earth as acid rain
The rain pollutes our green land
Look after what we have
The world is special, it is in our hands!

Reece Dugdale (12)
Hutton CE Grammar School, Preston

The Crying Hen

1 out of 1,000
I'm the only 1
All the hens gorge
Themselves but me
No, I know what
Happens in the
Slaughtering room.

You slice and dice
At our necks.
You show no fear
We walk around headless
With our blood pouring out
You just think we're happy
Being in 50cm cages
But no, you're wrong
You're killing all of us
So stop please.

Simon Theaker (12)
Hutton CE Grammar School, Preston

Don't Pollute

The world is a big place,
Full of pollution,
Hundreds of places polluting
All around the world,
From America to China.

In the form of fumes from cars,
Smoke from factories,
And so on.

There is a way to stop it,
Walk or ride a bike,
Instead of a car,
Recycle.

There are ways to help
So do it!

Alex Dell (12)
Hutton CE Grammar School, Preston

Terrorists

Just think for one moment
I hate them, it's not fair
They are innocent people
Who are dying
Why can they not just
Stop it?

They bombed the two
Biggest buildings in the world.
The Twin Towers
2,700 people died
All of them were innocent.
And loads of them
Had to jump out.

Jonny Wood (12)
Hutton CE Grammar School, Preston

65

Go Without!

I'm bare, along without water and food
Yet you are full, in company with water and food.
I'm not hungry, nor am I thirsty,
Yet you are still hungry and you are thirsty.

I'm living in darkness, yet I see the light.
You are basking in glory, yet darkness surely awaits
By hope of glistening tomorrow, is my saviour of today.
Your hopeless of a gloomy tomorrow is your shine of today.

Nabeel Shah (16)
Joseph Chamberlain College, Birmingham

Let's Make It Better . . .

People here, people there,
Breathe the same air.
We all share the same seas
All live in one land
People everywhere can learn how to
Work together, care together . . .
To make this world a better place!

Sabina Hussain (16)
Joseph Chamberlain College, Birmingham

Very Old Earth We Live In . . .

Our old Earth needs a helping hand
All we need to do is pick up . . . and throw it in the can
To keep the Earth fresh
To keep it clean
To keep it bright green
This very old Earth we live in needs our help.

Esminar Akhtar (16)
Joseph Chamberlain College, Birmingham

Who Are You?

It is that we know
Your pride, being a soldier
Killer or hero?

Farah Fazil (17)
Joseph Chamberlain College, Birmingham

My Green Poem

The Earth is dying
Burning up in flames
The waters are rising
It's not surprising
It's us to blame
We should be put to shame
Buy organic food
We really should
No more chemicals
Turn your thermostat down
Don't be a clown
Recycle your newspapers
Bottles, glass and cans
It's only a small step in our plans
People are cutting down the trees
Squishing the flowers and bees
Just be green
Don't make a scene.

Jennifer Pearson (13)
Kirkland High School, Methil

Atmosphere Poem

A brand new day
T ime to shine
M y, my
O ver there
S ave the seas
P ut rubbish in the bins
H elp our world
E very day
R emember you live on
E arth.

Courtney Mackie (13)
Kirkland High School, Methil

The Big Green Poem

Our only home is getting eaten away
by all of our waste we just throw away.
Turn down the heating, it's no big deal,
but your fate you might just seal.
Turn off the light, spare yourself another night.
The trees, the trees, we are killing
and the seas we are filling.
Stop the damage you are doing,
it's your life you're ensuring.

Rhys French (13)
Kirkland High School, Methil

The Plant

Look at the landfill, isn't it big?
It used to be a big field that we kids used to play in
But then one day a big digger came and took it all away.

The sun is too bright so switch off the lights
And let the sunshine in to save the plants from sunburn!

Don't drop your litter so the plants won't be bitter
So the poor animals don't go bye-bye
We want them to say hi-hi.

Shaunie Potter (13)
Kirkland High School, Methil

Wake Up Call!

The polar bear says, 'Ouch!'
The penguin says, 'What?'
The global warming is hurting us no doubt.
What is the matter with you, can't you see
Our home turning into the sea?
We are losing our friends and family,
Don't you have any humanity?
If not for us, think for yourselves,
Your future generations will only see toys of us on your shelves.
Make a difference now, when you have the chance,
Don't wait and let the problem enhance.
Fight the global warming and free us now,
Rather than waiting for Al Gore to show you when and how!
Act now before it's too late,
For God's sake, look at our state!
Come on, act now,
You'll still make a difference
Even though you started out a bit slow.
Don't wait for a fall,
This is your big wake up call!

Karan Ahluwalia (13)
Kulosaari Secondary School, Finland

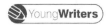

Corruption

Global warming kills,
We hear that every day.
But how are we to solve this crisis
And how much must we pay?

Dude, this stuff is complicated,
Maybe we should just leave it in the hands
Of the big, fat and wealthy
Oil corporate bands.

So what if these are the culprits,
Of melting the Arctic ice.
At least they have some taste,
And the pay they give is very nice.

So we conclude the oil business is not a dork,
And we are in no real mess.
So what if the flood waters have engulfed New York?
What's one town more or less?

So global warming kills,
But does that really matter?
So what if our policies,
Are madder than a hatter?

Welcome to politics.

Ville Syrjänen (14)
Kulosaari Secondary School, Finland

One Planet

Nature's beauty
Pollution, industry
All fades away.

It is not too late
Recycle, use less, love Earth
One planet, make it count.

Juhana Voutilainen (13)
Kulosaari Secondary School, Finland

When We Were Little

When we were little,
We used to play by this swing,
Next to this big tree,
Every single day.
When we were little,
You used to tell me your secrets
And I would tell you mine
And we would keep these secrets till the end of time.
When we were little,
It was always fun and games,
Nothing ever mattered to us either way,
Until you said goodbye,
The days went away,
Along with the fun and the games.
When we were little,
You said you'd never leave,
But you just broke your promise,
That you swore you would keep.
When we were little,
We never said goodbye.
Now I stand by our swing,
Alone in our favourite place
Because you decided to leave me in this hateful place.

Emily Sue Willis (17)
Kulosaari Secondary School, Finland

Littering

It's a shame that people litter,
Harm all the nature's little critters,
Even if you have a load of cash,
Don't think that you can trash,
Don't think it's not serious,
The environmentalists will be furious.

Olli Rekonen (15)
Kulosaari Secondary School, Finland

Earth

We love you
Don't fade away
All the bad
We have given away.
The words we speak of you are true.
You are our hero
The strongest and the bravest.

Wait, don't go away
We need you here to stay!
Please forgive us for our boldness,
We don't mean to show our coldness.

You are a true friend
A mother to all living.
A home you provide for all of us
Thus, away you shall not go,
You have strength, which is not to get low.

We love you
Don't go away!

Allegra Stodolsky (13)
Kulosaari Secondary School, Finland

What Else?

Ten or twelve years with Darfur
925 million people starving
The ozone layer, the ice in the Arctic
The biofuels, the greenhouse effect
The global warming
The overflowing of oceans
Millions drowned
My 14 years recently turned.

Gabriela Gonzalez Garcia (14)
Kulosaari Secondary School, Finland

Mother Earth

An olive tree that shelters
A city of cicadas
Our Mother Nature
And her beauty and her treasures.

People in their selfishness
Don't really even care
But Mother Earth deserves nothing less
Than our concern and dare.

Let's change the world together
Let's show everyone we care
Let's make the world better
Enjoy what she's got to share.

Gioanna Iacono (14)
Kulosaari Secondary School, Finland

Earth

I want them to notice how dirty I become each day
Because inside myself I feel so grey.
I want them to notice there's too much pollution
But they don't even think of a solution.
I want them to care about me
And not just live on me for free.
I want them to keep me clean
And notice my nature green.
I want them to recycle
And not just make carbon cycle.
I don't want to cry too much and spoil their fun
I just want them to have fun in the sun.

Ruchi Verma (13)
Kulosaari Secondary School, Finland

Nature's Doomsday

Five more minutes
Midnight is closer.

Five more minutes
Wars will be over.

All our mistakes will be forgiven
Our whole existence will be forgotten.

All our dreams will be blown away
Along with talk of 'it'll be okay'.

It's the last time I'm turning off this light
It's only five minutes to midnight.

Anna Auvinen (14)
Kulosaari Secondary School, Finland

Voices

A majestic green tower
draped with the scarves of decades
adorned with the jewels of seasons past.
A
magnificent
monument
to
the
passage
of time

Gone -
in one
fell swoop.
　　Desecrated by a flashing
metal blade.
Merciless
in its attack.

We cry
out.
We shriek
great pleas.
We yell
threats of police.
All for
naught.

Will our cries
ever be enough?
A louder voice
is surely needed
to drown out
the
damage.

Minerva Lim Shu Ching (14)
Methodist Girls' Secondary School, Singapore

75

Lonely World

A dark town,
The buildings are rundown,
The people sick,
The sky is dark and dusty,
A small child weeps,
Her mother has choked in the atmosphere,
In the dark town.

A dry world,
The seas are polluted,
The animals are dead,
Africa is fading fast,
An elephant wails,
She is lost and alone,
In the dry world.

Is this the world in a millennium?
Is it the end of our race?
If we do not act in time
This is our future,
So say *no!*
And change today . . .
And save our world.

Isabelle Harrison (11)
Notre Dame High School, Norwich

What It Could Be?

The sun is shining,
The wind is blowing,
The rain is falling,
The grass is growing.

Pollution is rising,
Trees are falling,
Waste is growing,
The world is dying.

Muirin Keating (11)
Notre Dame High School, Norwich

Now Is The Time To Change

Our planet, our world, our home,
The place that we all know,
The place that we have grown up in,
Well that's about to go.

The world isn't staying the same you know,
I know that's hard to believe,
But with all the damage you're doing,
Our lovely planet is going to leave!

Did you ever hear the ice caps are melting?
England is no longer cold!
Africa is stuck in poverty,
Now is the time to be bold!

Now is the time to take action,
Doing your little bit,
Could actually save the planet,
Whatever you do, don't quit.

Change your house, it's possible,
Change your lifestyle too,
Recycle all your rubbish
It's actually quite easy to do.

Alice Chancellor (12)
Notre Dame High School, Norwich

We Must Act

Greenhouse gases
Polluting our world.
The factories
Pumping out masses of smoke,
Killing our world.
The ice caps are melting,
We must act now.
It's not too late
Before the Earth cracks.

Mark Kirwan (11)
Notre Dame High School, Norwich

You Are Not Alone

Say no to litter,
It is bad,
The rain goes pitter-patter,
The floods make me sad.

The world is dying,
They say they've done no wrong,
But I know they're lying,
Pollution has a smelly pong.

Polar bears, elephants,
Birds and whales,
They're all dying,
In the powerful gales.

We are killing our home,
It's the only one we own,
So treasure it dearly,
Don't worry, you are not alone.

Bethany Hodson (11)
Notre Dame High School, Norwich

Saving Our World

Look what we've done to our planet,
It really is a mess,
But we can try to stop it,
So we must try our best.

Pollution and destroying the environment,
Are just a few things,
They're destroying our planet,
They're destroying the ozone rings.

Reduce, recycle, reuse,
Save electricity, save gas,
Go by train, go by bus,
Go to work without polluting en mass.

Pippa Beard
Notre Dame High School, Norwich

Let's Save The Planet

Let's save the hammerheads,
Let's save the bats,
Let's save the guinea pigs,
Let's save the cats.

Let's save the cacti,
Let's save the trees,
Let's save the flowers too and
Let's save the leaves.

Will climate change get any worse,
Can it really, can it?
So, don't just stand there,
Let's save the planet!

Eve McGrady & Rosina Kavanagh (11)
Notre Dame High School, Norwich

The Land Of Cheese

Roses are red, violets are blue,
Plants are green
And you should be too!

Charles Pettit (12) & Joey Santori (11)
Notre Dame High School, Norwich

Recycle

R euse the old things to make new things.
E ventually makes new things.
C ash can be given when you recycle your admission.
Y our litter counts.
C are for your environment.
L ove your environment, recycle more.
E nvironmentally friendly.

Katie Betts
Our Lady & St Chad's Sports College, Wolverhampton

Rainforests

R is for rain that trickles on the leaves
A is for all the little animals from ants, bees and monkeys
I is for insects flying and crawling all around
N is for new roots and plants that spring up here and there
F is for forests! Please save our beautiful trees
O is for orang-utans that swing from branch to branch
R is for river that runs deep into the valley
E is for endangered species, soon could all be lost
S is for save our animals, plants and trees
T is for take the time to care for our forest.

Amiee Felton
Our Lady & St Chad's Sports College, Wolverhampton

Keep Your Environment Tidy!

Recycle all your junk
And you won't be a punk,
If you get rid of your trash
You might earn a little cash.
Throw your litter in the bins
And recycle all your tins,
School isn't very far
So you don't need your car.

Eleanor Francis
Our Lady & St Chad's Sports College, Wolverhampton

Recycle, Recycle

Recycle the junk you've got instead of chucking it away.
If you do, it could even pay.
Recycle all the stuff and get it out the way.
You can do a lot with yourself.
Even some of us recycle like a happy elf.
You've got the power to save your health.
You have to save the planet
Before the planet is gone forever.

Ben Bryant
Our Lady & St Chad's Sports College, Wolverhampton

Anybody Can Recycle

Everyone can get rid of junk,
Even if you are a monk.
Take off your mask,
If you do this you will be great,
And you'll get another mate.
All you have to do is recycle.

Eden Da Costa
Our Lady & St Chad's Sports College, Wolverhampton

Peace And Blood

You say love, they say peace
Then why can I see people crying
And two minutes later you see them dying?
You say love and they say peace
But all I see is blood and beef.
Can I ask you,
Why do I see children dying and families crying
If you say love and they say peace?
But I don't see any of this!

Dalia Ulanowska (13)
St Mary's CE High School, Hendon

Animals, Crimes And Our Lives

Why kill an animal?
Why kill a person?
It's not helping you . . .
It'll live on your conscience.

The world will end one day
And it'll all be sad.
The taste of emptiness
Will float in our lives.

Don't think about hate
But think about love.
Look around you . . .
And think again.

It's not just about you,
It's about all of us.
I know you think it's OK
But you're just kidding yourself.

People's lives are in a game
No shame we're all dead.
It's a human you're talking about
Not a thing . . . but a life.

And there as I began
Animal or human
It's all part of our lives . . .
It's affecting our lives . . .

Luiza Salciuc (13)
St Mary's CE High School, Hendon

Why Fight? Why Bomb?
Why Can't We Get Along?

War, war, can't you go away,
Just leave it for another day?
Why fight? Why bomb?
Why can't we just get along?
Racism, poverty and war,
Poverty is basically people being poor.
Why fight? Why bomb?
Why can't we just get along?
War is killing people and it's not nice,
Why can't it just melt away like a block of ice?
'Cause it is taking people's lives.
Why fight? Why bomb?
Why can't we get along?
Racism is bad so why do it?
So why don't you just stop it
And do your little bit?
Why fight? Why bomb?
Why can't we just get along?

James Gibson (12)
St Mary's CE High School, Hendon

Murder! Murder!

Knives are harmful
But still people use them
They cause anger, frustration and pain
For comfort and protection
But out comes murder and bleeding.

They laugh, then they cry
What is going on?
The hate, it wasn't just a silly mistake
They did it on purpose
Murder! Murder!

Nadia Daniel (11)
St Mary's CE High School, Hendon

War

War, war, war,
Where do I begin?
If you ask me,
It's nothing but a sin.

People all over the world,
Filled with fears,
Next thing you know,
Their eyes are drowned in tears.

Sending out your loved ones,
Where there's guns and bombs,
Some time later,
Your loved ones will be gone.

So if you disagree with this,
Then why don't you please,
Everyone hold your hands up,
For the London Week of Peace.

Tegan Johnson (13)
St Mary's CE High School, Hendon

What Is War?

War.
War is death,
Sadness and loneliness,
That is war.
War.
War is destruction,
Havoc and killing,
A drop of blood,
Heartbreaking news to families,
That is war.
War will bring an end
To life as we know it.
That is what war will do.

Ervin Haxhiaj (13)
St Mary's CE High School, Hendon

Where's It Gonna End?

Put down the guns,
Put down the knives,
Everybody just make peace
And live your lives.
Every day somebody dies,
Leaving their families crying behind.
Life's too short for all this pain,
So put down the weapons and start again.

We were raised in the streets and the gutter,
But we still learn to love one another,
We've got brothers killing each other,
This is the life we live,
Life is what you make it,
So you gotta make it worthwhile,
Don't know what tomorrow brings,
Have you ever thought, where's it gonna end?

Tianne Youngsam (13)
St Mary's CE High School, Hendon

All Disasters

The war makes us lonely, sad and helpless,
Mostly sad for losing friends and family.
All the brave people along the journey,
All dying very early.

Bombs, killings, blood,
People lying dead in the mud,
Trying to take cover,
Let's not make it another.

Poverty, homeless, poor,
Let's not make more.
It's not fair,
That people don't care.

Jose Oliveira (12)
St Mary's CE High School, Hendon

All The Problems In The World

Gun and knife crime
It makes me scared
Children getting killed
It's just not fair.

Pollution in the seas
Rivers and lakes
Fish and birds
Dying for no sake.

Starvation all over the world
No food or drink
Their cries can't be heard.

Global warming
Hurricanes and tornadoes
Floods in Trinidad and Tobago.

Keahana Miller (11)
St Mary's CE High School, Hendon

Racism, Full Stop!

Racism
Discrimination
Racism
Disliking
Racism
Cruelty
Racism
Brutality
Racism
Ain't reality
Racism . . .
Full stop!

Tania Mousinho (13)
St Mary's CE High School, Hendon

Problems In The World

People are homeless,
They don't have a place to stay.
It makes the world look like a mess,
I feel sorry for them, I have to say.
People are starving,
They haven't got any food.
Children just walk past and laugh,
Which is absolutely rude.
People are sick,
They haven't got anything to cure them.

Dominique Fajembola (11)
St Mary's CE High School, Hendon

Cloudless

It's a peaceful mission.
Take away the black and grey.
Make a cloudless world.
Be confident.
Let's make friends with enemies.
Explore the feeling.
The operation of loving life.
Make a new term.
Bring a smile . . .

Djoana Smirnova (13)
St Mary's CE High School, Hendon

Between Us

Between us we share love and passion
Despite the brutal and sad reactions,
I'll continue to love her all my days
No matter what he or she may say.
Despite my paler skin complexion,
This love is true without deception.
We're still chocolate, I'm just white and she's dark
And the more our families continue to bark,
Nothing will come between us.

Adeorike Oshinyemi (13)
St Mary's CE High School, Hendon

Where Is The Peace?

Where is the peace?
It's just a crease
In the civilisation
The evil's ruling
The good is cruel
The world is crawling for help
Where is the peace?

Amy Lindsay (13)
St Mary's CE High School, Hendon

Bad Habits

In the last year knife crime has gone up by miles here
It has to stop or you'll find yourself with a cop.

Drugs, drugs, drugs, they're like little bugs,
When you take them for the first time
This is a huge, huge crime.

Ricky Drew (11)
St Mary's CE High School, Hendon

The Thoughts I Want To Spread

I stare out of the window
I look at the stars
I wonder what the world will become
With all those factories and cars.

Come on, I think. Remember,
Think about the past
When environment came first
And money came last.

I do not say that we must stop
All the progress in the world
But we should stop pollution
Or what else will the future hold?

The most important thing isn't lipstick
And neither is polish for your nails
Save these ten Euros
And think about the whales!

We say that all those factories
Give out just a tiny bit of smog
And all that paper that we waste
Is just a little log!

But instead of excuses
Why won't we just economise?
And the number of those factories
I suggest should be minimised.

I'm only suggesting,
I can't order you about.
But I'm quite sure that this will help.
I almost have no doubt!

Evgeniya Mamulova (13)
St Mary's School, Cyprus

The Complaints Of A Tree

I am a tree
Near the sea
Safe on an island
On Hawaii.

Every morning on the radio
I hear the news
Bad news
From every nation.

People cutting down trees
Killing forests
What else
Will the future hold?

I hear them speaking about recycling
I wonder, do they do it?
Not at all
It's just words.

They keep talking on and on about our benefits
Which they call boring science
But do they appreciate them?
Not at all.

We are the ones that make the world green
With our bright leaves
We are the ones that give fresh air
Full of oxygen, nothing else.

I hope all of you
In the near future
Will help in saving us
From pure death.

Nemat Hamezeh (13)
St Mary's School, Cyprus

Will It Ever Go Away?

Life is evil and hard
I can never drop my guard
I roam around the streets all day
Looking for a place to stay.

My usual corner of the park is taken
When I finally sleep I am woken
To find a small boy holding money
He calls me by the name 'Mummy'.

I'm too desperate to care
For life is so unfair
So I quickly grab what isn't mine
To find in my hand some coins, there are nine.

Being homeless is a crime
Because we haven't a dime
So we have no chance of a good life
Instead we kill, mainly with a knife.

We need money to live
Unfortunately there's not enough left to give
However much we try
We can never find out why.

But I believe that in our heart
We find it difficult to part
From the badness in the world today
That will hopefully go away.

Alexandra Myrianthous (13)
St Mary's School, Cyprus

Our Dying Planet Rap

Our planet's dying man,
Can't you see it?

If you can't
Try to feel it!

Smelly fuels, they just won't do,
Most of them smell like rotting poo!

Massive factories producing more waste,
Something else horrid for fish to taste!

Cutting down trees for furniture,
Murdering animals to take their fur!

Are we jealous of these poor creatures?
I guess we are, to strip them of their features!

Use solar energy for your house,
Don't put poison down and spare that mouse!

You can't do it, you just have to try,
For instance, admire the beauty of a butterfly!

If we don't do something for the Earth
It won't take anymore and just burst!

Nicolas Panayiotou (13)
St Mary's School, Cyprus

Litter, What Can We Do?

Litter, litter, what can we do?
You ruin our countries and cities don't you?
You are everywhere, we can't get away.
You even pollute the place where we play.

We should put our rubbish in the bin.
To help us not be in the sin.
Do this so we will be safe.
To make our world a better place.

Jaskiran Rai (11)
Smestow School, Wolverhampton

War Is The End

War is a dangerous, dark ogre
that fills our tales with bombs and killings.
War is a mad, drunk beast
that looms, country to country
destroying buildings and damaging houses.
War is an aggressive sea storm
that never gives up tossing the poor ship up and down.
War is anger and hate
wandering in forests late at night
shooting and stabbing innocent children.
War is a sinful dare devil
murdering hundreds, thousands and millions.
War is misfortune
like a terrorist throwing violence throughout the country.
War is a deadly nightmare
where children scream and terror pours throughout the land.
War is an inconvenient monster
disturbing married couples and ecstatic families.
War is a dagger
ripping through flesh.
War is end, end of family laughter
and fortunate events.

Harkeran Jandu (12)
Smestow School, Wolverhampton

Big Green Trees

Killing nature's habitat is not good.
They might die without a home.
Don't chop down trees.
Recycle old paper, it is much more fun.
Without trees there will be no oxygen to breathe
So we will die without them.
Some trees provide fruit that we eat
Also some animals eat them too.

Kristie Wheeler (11)
Smestow School, Wolverhampton

93

Not For Long

The sky is blue
But not for long.
The way we're going there will be no song.
We destroy our planet piece by piece,
Stop it now
For heaven's sake.
I'm all alone,
I can't do it on my own.
Help the planet, help it now.
We are destroying the world,
Stop the pollution
While you've got a chance.
Bike ride,
Use cars less,
Think of the environment now!
It may be fun, it may be cool
For all I've done is show you to the door.
Recycle,
It's the lifecycle.

Holly Taylor (11)
Smestow School, Wolverhampton

Recycle Litter Before It Bins You!

Litter is a terrible, rotten monster
Made of all the rubbish of the world.
It seeks to cover the world
With its horrid contents,
Suffocating the Earth slowly.

Litter is a tidal wave
Sucking all the rubbish up
As the tide goes in, making it grow.
Litter brings disaster, chaos and mess.
To defeat don't chuck it, *recycle it!*

Sophie Horton (12)
Smestow School, Wolverhampton

War, The Enemy Of The Earth

Bombs, explosions, guns
Planes fly by
Terrorists fight
Guns shoot
Bombs explode.

No one surrenders
Bombs like thunder
Live to tell a tale
Tanks roll across like an angry rhino
Soldiers march
Destruction and devastation.

People get injured and get shot
But they fight back
Hiding in buildings
Fighting from high
Might get cut down
But they will still fight.
It must stop!

Nathan Timmins (11)
Smestow School, Wolverhampton

War Is Bad

W ar can result in devastation.
A ftermaths can result in civil war.
R acism. War can divide countries.

I solation. Some countries get isolated in war.
S tarvation. Some countries lose crops in war.

B loodshed all over the world.
A fghanistan. Look what happened there after war.
D eath. Innocent people die in war.

Do you want this in your world?

Freddie Sanders (11)
Smestow School, Wolverhampton

Recycling!

Bins smell damp, rotting, decomposing, decaying,
It's brown, squishy, mushy and wet.
Sounds of trucks, rumbling noisily,
Dirt everywhere, smelly van,
A message on the side,
Banging and clashing of bottles and cans,
Like thunder and lightning.

Wearing yellow vests to stand out from the rest,
Recycling is environmentally friendly.
Reuse your plastic shopping bags,
Recycle all your packaging. There is too much now.

Best things to recycle!

Paper bags, scraps and newspapers,
Clothes can be recycled by going to charity shops,
Garden waste in the green bin,
Only use water that's needed,
So we can save the world!

Gabriella Bueno Del Carpio (11)
Smestow School, Wolverhampton

Start Recycling Now!

If you want to see our world be bright,
Then start recycling for more light,
Cans, tins, plastic, jars, glass, whatever,
Most people in our world recycle never,
Stop making a horrible smell go around,
Also a noisy sound,
Start turning off taps to save water,
Stop making our world from being shorter,
Give clothes to charity, don't throw them away
Or something will happen one day,
Do the world a favour,
Start recycling *now!*

Sadé Thompson (11)
Smestow School, Wolverhampton

A Can With A Message In It

I am a shiny aluminium can
That has been drunk by a boy
I have been chucked in a green box
That can be recycled into a toy.

I have been put into a van
With a message on the side to say
'If you recycle me I'll be your no 1 fan'.

I have loads of friends in the recycling centre
They all get taken into a bin
Which can be recycled into a new tin
Making the world a better place!

Mostly everything we use we recycle
Glass, cans, paper and plastic
Can be made into something new
Which is really fantastic.

Jessica Kelly (11)
Smestow School, Wolverhampton

Pollution

The Earth is a dustbin,
Always full of litter,
Never a tidy place,
Making the world a depressing and gloomy place.

The world is turning into a mouthful of smoke
As if you've just taken a drag from a cigarette,
Always smoky and suffocating,
Never a time when the smoke isn't in your face.

So next time you go for a journey,
Think, think, think,
Try to reduce the amount of pollution,
Catching the bus, walking or riding your bike,
Just think, you're killing the world.

Mitchell Partridge (11)
Smestow School, Wolverhampton

97

Identity

I'm black, I'm white, I'm brown.
That's our names.
I've been called that since Year 5.
I've just been called it.
We don't know how they came.
We are not like the others.
We are always feeling down.
It really hurts, it really does.
Is it better than being hurt?
If one person starts, they all start.
If one person stops, they all stop.
We're fine now, happy not sad, but happy.
Now we're like everyone else.
I'm Amma, I'm Holly, I'm Sahara,
That's our names.

Sahara Pudden (11)
Smestow School, Wolverhampton

Animals In The Forest

The animals that live in the forest
Look so sweet and honest,
But then the big strong men come along
And destroy the birds' song.

All the cars go rushing by
And all the animals stop and die,
All the predators stop and think
Where's my prey to complete my link?

All the animals go into the city
There to search for pity,
Instead of nice, dense and soft earth
Well-covered in concrete and moss
To now forever dwell in broken dreams
And lost habitats.

Rhys Biddle-Jones (11)
Smestow School, Wolverhampton

War Is . . .

Tanks and machines,
Tanks are powerful.

Men are loyal,
Men are rogues.

Leaders are kind,
Leaders are greedy.

Bombs go *boom!*
Bombs go *bang!*

War is war,
I don't know why,
Stop it now
Before we die!

Chris Mainwaring (12)
Smestow School, Wolverhampton

Pollution

Pollution these days is getting worse and worse,
I wish I could just let out all my anger to the world.
Maybe we need to cut down on electricity,
Maybe we need to recycle more?
Stop using cars and instead use buses.
What should we do?
We need to save this awesome world.

Look at the polar bears in the Arctic,
They're going to be extinct soon,
That shouldn't happen
If we save our planet!
People don't want to live in a hazardous waste dump,
So act now!

Gage Naylor (12)
Smestow School, Wolverhampton

Rainforest

Rainforest, rainforest all chopped down
Rainforest, rainforest, a saw-like death itself
Rainforest, rainforest where have you gone?
You give us our life
And we should give you yours
You are disappearing, not reappearing
Help me now
Be so brave
Join my quest
To save our friends
If you can help
Use both sides of the paper
Be the trees' recreator.

Tijana Nicolaou-Samuels (11)
Smestow School, Wolverhampton

Recycling

Woken up suddenly by the sound of clashing bins,
Looking through the window,
Binmen chucking empty tins,
What a waste, all done in haste.

Eating breakfast,
An empty cereal box is thrown away,
Put it in the recycling bin,
No time to delay.

At school, in art,
Cutting pieces of paper,
So we do our part
And recycle leftover pieces later.

Simren Johal (11)
Smestow School, Wolverhampton

Recycling

Black bins, green bins
And brown bins too,
All these bins,
I don't know what to do!

Make sure you recycle,
Learn what you have to do,
The telly and the Internet,
Will show you if you haven't a clue.

Cardboard, glass, tins and clothes,
I'm sure you can use again,
Put them in the bins outside
And save the environment!

Gemma Fereday (12)
Smestow School, Wolverhampton

Making The World A Better Place

Saving the world is a very helpful thing,
Recycling cans, newspapers into recycling bins.
Clashing, banging and smashing at local centres,
Giving old clothes to poor unwealthy people,
Making them happy and feeling peaceful.
Rotting grass, dead flowers and leaves,
This garden waste can also be recycled in garden waste bins.
Compost heaps are great for rotting potato peel and banana skins.
After a while they will rot and disappear,
So recycle and make this world a better place.

Pooja Mahey (11)
Smestow School, Wolverhampton

The Litterbug

I'm a piece of litter as small as a mouse,
Getting kicked and thrown about as if I'm not useful.
Soon I will be as big and as wide as the universe,
But I am useful.
You can do all sorts of stuff with me
Like recycle me or make a robot with me.
It's amazing that me, a piece of small litter,
Can make big things happen, if you help.
So what you gonna do,
Stop it, still drop it or hop it?

Chloe-May Forrest (11)
Smestow School, Wolverhampton

Pollution Is All Around Us

We hear about it everywhere . . .
Birds splattered with oil, wailing as if they are in pain,
Car fumes all around us, helping to cause global warming,
Energy, we waste a lot of it, all the time,
Factories always belting smoke into the air,
So, if we just cut down on using cars,
Stop factories belting so much smoke out,
Stop wasting too much energy,
Help the birds in pain,
The world would be a better place.

Hannah Moss (11)
Smestow School, Wolverhampton

The Bin Men Lorry In The Morning

Bang, clatter, crash!
The binmen have come at last.
We fill up the bins
And they take them away
And they empty it out into their big lorry.

Clink, smash goes the glass,
Mixed in well with the trash.
Smelly garbage, rotting waste,
Everything is out of date.

Molly Sugar Brown Hale (11)
Smestow School, Wolverhampton

The War

War is as horrible as broccoli,
Explosions, weapons, killing and mines,
Tanks and scary trenches,
HQs and markers
You move and no stopping.

So a message to all of you,
Wars are horrible,
Don't get involved,
But help any way you can.

Ashley Davies (12)
Smestow School, Wolverhampton

Recycling

Recycling is so fun,
You want to do it more,
When you start you can't ever stop,
When the binmen come and take it all,
You want to do it again and again.

Gurjot Bains (11)
Smestow School, Wolverhampton

The Pollution Solution

This is pollution, it's killing wildlife.
It's killing the world and it just doesn't know it
So pick it up and don't just throw it.
There's rubbish everywhere and we just don't care.
The ice caps are melting and we're helping.
Cars keep going but we won't stop throwing.
Car fumes are killing and they just keep spilling.

Cavan Walters (11)
Smestow School, Wolverhampton

Pollution Poem

This is pollution and it's killing evolution
Pollution is mad and it's getting bad
Binmen are coming, we've got so much rubbish
Try to clean it up or we are going to get done
The ice caps are melting and it's really not helping
The animals are dropping and the cows keep plopping
Plastic bags are dropping and we're not recycling.

Mark Thursby (12)
Smestow School, Wolverhampton

Endangered Animals

Hunters are always hunting for fur, tusks and more.
Animals get caught in nets and wrappings.
Polar bears are now endangered
Because of all the climate change.
Polar bears, tigers, whales too,
They're all endangered because of you.

Tasara Charlie Taylor (11)
Smestow School, Wolverhampton

Drop It In The Bin!

Litter is everywhere, but no one cares.
Put it in the bin, do not sin.
Think about the animals.
Nah, you just don't care.
There are bins everywhere
So pop it in and just don't drop it.

Joe Guy (12)
Smestow School, Wolverhampton

Recycle Me

Wait and see
What you get back from me.
Make a newspaper,
Make a chair.
Thank you for recycling,
Come back again.

Nathan Sankey (11)
Smestow School, Wolverhampton

Pollution

Pollution is a killer massacring the world at night.
Pollution is a mass murderer to the world and us.
Pollution is a pillow smothering the Earth.
Pollution is factories pumping black smoke into the air.
Pollution is millions of cars on the M6 suffocating the Earth.
Pollution is CO_2 gases pumping into the air.

Bradley Townley (11)
Smestow School, Wolverhampton

River Of Love

They hissed and spat at her soul
Shredding it to pieces
She cried
Drenching her soul
Putting out her glow of faith
Her sparkle of love
Why, from where was this pain coming?
And why here, on the shoulders of the world
That was already falling from the lack of love
Hope
Forgiveness
Faith
And love?
The girl pleaded to God for the answer
He answered her in a loving breeze
Blowing away the heavy cloud
Whispering in her ear
You have love
You have faith
And you have me
This is your time, now go
With those words she was lifted so high
She danced with the stars
Her glow of faith turned into a sun
So that no one had to be lost in the dark
And her sparkle of love turned
Into a crystal clear river of love
So that no one has to suffer one drop of hate.

Zoe Polson (12)
The European School, Costa Rica

106

A Poem Of Home

When you are at home
So happy, enjoying life with electricity
Someone else is suffering
I am not talking about a human
I am talking about trees and animals
Living things we do not know that they live
They have a heart, mind and feelings that we do not mind
When animals search for a home
What they find is only ground and seeds
We can help cutting one, putting two
Together we can do it
It is our problem
It is our fault
It is our home
Our world so sad
Our world so bad
We can hear his cry every day
Just close your eyes and listen
And you will see how much damage you've done.

Felipe García (12)
The European School, Costa Rica

The Earth

The Earth is a beautiful place,
We have to take care of it every day.
We have to stop contamination,
Trash everywhere.
You are destroying this Earth!

Make it a better place . . .
Where we save energy,
Cut no trees
And live very happily!

Daniela Vargas (12)
The European School, Costa Rica

107

Earth's Evil

Black wings,
Red eyes,
Feeding up on all the evil we do,
Big claws that grasp the Earth, ruling it,
Is Earth going to end up as that?
A world ruled by evil?

It spreads on Earth like spilled ink on paper,
And we still don't stop it,
This evil is social, and it enters people's hearts
And makes them disrespectful, raged and unconscious,
It smells like hot steam filled with the sourness of the lemon,
And sounds like a dog's bark.

It's not too late to stop Earth's evil,
Every heart that you've hurt, go and mend it,
Respect the people around you,
Come on!
Help us stop Earth's evil from spreading,
Help us make it disappear.

Maria Fernanda (12)
The European School, Costa Rica

Trash? No Way!

Today I was walking down the street
And saw some trash below my feet
I hurried away, with a little frown
Whoever dumped that trash was such a clown!

As I walked, I saw trash here and there
What now is so clear was once so rare
So while the sun is still bright and the grass is still green
Please everyone keep this world clean!

Andrea Duarte (13)
The European School, Costa Rica

Stop Hurting Our Earth

Global warming,
Animals are frowning.
Lots of gases from cars
And companies,
There is no recycling.

Don't cut any trees down
And please don't throw trash
On the ground.

Paper with paper,
Glass with glass,
Plastic with plastic,
It's fantastic!

Don't give excuses,
Help the animals like the moose,
Polar bears, penguins and the goose.

Can't you see, we are
Hurting our Earth?

Hildegard Kahle Sagot (13)
The European School, Costa Rica

Apartheid

Black and whites
Were separated
There was injustice, discrimination, unfairness
Black people had rage
Had courage to riot
And were against the police.
They wanted their freedom
Black people didn't want
To serve white people.

The ANC (African National Congress)
Was a great organisation
For riots and strikes
They wanted black and white people
On the same side
And wanted to accomplish things with peace!

Maria Camila Fonseca (13)
The European School, Costa Rica

Recycling

It is easy
It's not hard
I will tell you what it's all about.
You only need to take all the things
That can be reused in your house,
Then you take it to this place
And you will be amazed with all the things you will see.
And there I will be, putting what you brought in the bin.
Only by doing this we can help the environment!
It is very easy
It's not hard
So why are people not smart?

Mónica Gómez (12)
The European School, Costa Rica

Earth

We humans should think a little bit more
about what is happening with the Earth,
take responsibility for what is occurring.
People cut trees and do not think about the effects of doing that,
we kill trees by doing that, trees clean the Earth.
In the other parts of the world some parts of the Earth
are warming up because of the global warming,
everything is because of the actions that we make.
We should take responsibility for what is going to happen,
if we still do not care what is going to happen to the Earth.
So please take care of every action that you do,
you have two options: help the Earth or let her die little by little.

Lisa Lin Wu (13)
The European School, Costa Rica

Clean Your Environment

Work hard to scrub your environment,
Clean and neat,
Leave no room for rats.

Clean dirty pots and pans,
Let them shine,
Cut every bush around.

Stop refuse bins from building a castle,
Wash every pail and bowl,
Sweep every nook and cranny.

Stop all pits and holes from growing,
Stop pests from rejoicing,
Stop diseases from clapping and dancing.

Keep no refuse on any spot,
Don't be a dirty and unpleasant fellow,
Do not look shabby in your looks.

Ozoeze Onyinye Ada (13)
The International School of Ibadan, Nigeria

Wage War Against Violence

Here,
Seconds have turned to minutes,
Minutes gradually changed to hours,
Hours have gone by,
Years have rolled by,
Decades have passed,
Centuries have also gone by,
And still day by day,
Man becomes his own enemy,
The world is distraught.
The wonderful bright scenes of the world,
Have been stained due to Man's greed,
And the Earth shed tears, for being stained.
By the blood clots of saints and innocents,
Who die in violence and wars.
Let's wage war against violence,
For in this world, we are tenants,
Dwelling in huts,
Soon, very soon, death will come for the whole world,
Huts will become dilapidated and will fall,
And the world will come to an end,
In weakness over the Earth
The whole world will rot,
And we, who lived in a world of violence,
Will be identified and seen as -
Wastes.

Shafiu Olaitan Aminah (13)
The International School of Ibadan, Nigeria

Pollution

Pollution here,
Pollution there
Pollution everywhere.

Turn around
Without a sound
Choking people
On the ground.

Pollution here,
Pollution there,
Pollution everywhere.

Every boat has got its sail
To keep it above the water's tail
But the whale he had no fear . . .
Until pollution came so near.

Pollution here,
Pollution there,
Pollution.

Adegoke Adetola (13)
The International School of Ibadan, Nigeria

War

War, aimless destruction,
Of lives and properties,
Causing great poverty.
War, a wicked destroyer,
That causes great fear to the nation.
It makes people die,
And many people cry.
It symbolises enmity,
In the countries.
Lives were lost in the First World War,
Many more were forgotten in the Second World War.
If we stop this destruction,
We will have a peaceful nation,
And make everywhere green,
Like a paradise.
Let's stop war
So we will have a glorious world
As the 'Eden' above.

Omolawal Ayomide Oyindamola (13)
The International School of Ibadan, Nigeria

War!

Oh Africa
When will you stop the war?
People die
Families separate
People become disabled
Valuable things become destroyed
Treasure of the nation falls
Future of people is destroyed
Oh war, go away
We don't want you
You are just a tempest from the Devil
You should not be allowed to complete your mission
Let there be peace
Dear Africa
Let us be one
As a nation, then peace shall reign.

Alayande Mariam Temitope (12)
The International School of Ibadan, Nigeria

The Causes Of Wars

The causes of wars
Are struggles, brawls and lust
But to stop it all,
You should be just.

When war stands
Then peace stands still
To regain peace
End the war.

To end the war,
You need some words
Like please and why,
Can't this stop?

Egbokhare Olohi (13)
The International School of Ibadan, Nigeria

A Beauty To Behold

The big green tree and the beautiful flowers
How they show God's wonderful work.
How they make my heart rejoice
What a beauty to behold.

The big green tree and the beautiful flowers
They are friends to the lonely ones.
They protect my house from the hurricane
They give home to the chirping birds and the homeless squirrels
How kind and merciful they are.

How pale the world would be without the big green tree and the
beautiful flowers
How I dreamt my dreams, that deforestation was a dream, were real
And I would wake up to see that deforestation was never here
And the world would be a beauty to behold.

Uwalaka Merlin (12)
The International School of Ibadan, Nigeria

An Electrifying Encounter
At The Manda Hill Robots

I sat in my car
Waiting for the robots to turn green.
As my eyes swept across the road,
I noticed a boy, about my age,
Dressed in nothing but tatters.
He looked rather thin
And tired too!
Yet, his eyes were alive
Like a live electric wire;
Charged with hope.
He was putting up yet another poster
And it read, 'Sata - Man of Action'.
The boy's bold stare made a statement:
'One day, my life will be better'.
I admired his dauntless courage.

As the robot turned orange, our eyes met
And my lips automatically broke into a smile.
He smiled back at me.
We understood each other perfectly.
I could sense what he sensed:
'A better world is not too far off'.
I understood that the big day of change is just round the corner.

As the car sped off in response to the green signal
I decided to write this poem,
To make that encounter remain in my mind evergreen.

Meena Murugappan (14)
The International School of Lusaka, Zambia

Without A Place To Call Home

The rain started thundering,
Shaking the trees.
And the winds started howling,
At our quivering knees.

We sat there in silence, without a place to call home.

We looked at the sky,
Gaping and black.
We're such tiny men,
As the stars came back.

We sat there in silence, without a place to call home.

Huddled by the fire,
We fed from its heat.
Warmth settled over us,
Like a comforting sheet.

We sat there in silence, without a place to call home.

Numbing every joint,
The cold seeped through,
Furiously trembling,
As the coldness grew.

We sat there in silence, without a place to call home.

We could only rely,
Upon others that passed.
To give us the money,
So our hope would last.

We sat there in silence, without a place to call home.
The fire was out, so was all hope.

Sarah Brereton (11)
The Ladies' College, Guernsey

118

Rainforests

They're really half a world away,
There's nothing we can do.
'Rainforests' might be just one word
To kids like me and you.

They're really somewhere over there.
I may not even see
A rainforest in my entire life.
What should it mean to me?

I know that in these rainforests
That I may never see,
Half the world's plants, animals and insects
Live in harmony.

I know that trees are being cut,
Faster than we know.
These trees are where the creatures live,
So now where will they go?

So I know they're half a world away,
Rainforests I can't see.
But I can learn and understand
Because the future starts with me!

You can make a difference.

Eleanor Curzon Green (11)
The Ladies' College, Guernsey

We Need To Do Something

Please save the world,
Don't drop litter,
Turn off your taps,
Use renewable energy,
Just remember,
We need to do something.

Please save the world,
Reuse your plastic bags,
Grow your own food,
Stop polluting the Earth,
Just remember,
We need to do something.

Please save the world,
Don't shoot for fun,
Change to green,
Don't watch so much television,
Just remember,
We need to do something.

Please save the world,
Walk or cycle around,
Join an eco-committee,
Reduce your carbon footprint,
Just remember,
We need to do something.

Please save the world,
If we do it now,
Everything will change,
Recycle, reduce and reuse,
Just remember,
We need to do something.

Lucy Illingworth (11)
Wellington School, Ayr

Eco Wellies!

What can we do?
We can reuse, reduce and recycle,
Stop polluting our sky,
Use your eyes and see why,
Our planet needs our help.
What could you do?

What can we do?
Touch a switch, save a life,
Use a green bag for goods,
Try your best to be good,
Our planet needs our help.
What could you do?

What can we do?
Save energy!
Let a baby see a polar bear,
Don't let the planet go bare.
Our planet needs our help.
What could you do?

What can we do?
Reduce waste!
Use the bag all the time,
It's not a crime.
Our planet needs our help.
What could you do?

What can we do?
Put rubbish in a bin,
Do your best,
It's not a pest.
Our planet needs our help.
Get out there, do something!

Sophie Graham (12)
Wellington School, Ayr

Just Go Green

Save the Earth, this beautiful place
Or you will shame the human race,
Don't drop litter,
Don't shoot for fun,
All the animals will be done.
Go green, go green galore!

Lend a hand,
Every man,
Use a renewable source,
Turn off all lights,
You only need them at night.
Go green, go green galore!

Turn off your taps,
Make your own baps,
Walk or cycle around,
Grab the bus,
Stop the fuss.
Go green, go green galore!

Reduce, recycle, reuse,
Wear that old pair of shoes,
You've heard it, so obey it,
Only buy clothes
When you need more of those.
Go green, go green galore!

Remember all this,
Don't you dare dis,
All those good people out there,
Listen to these rules,
Stop using all our fuels.
Go green, go green galore!

Kennedy Cameron (11)
Wellington School, Ayr

Environmental Issues

Start growing your own food
Don't shoot animals for fun
Walk, cycle, just don't drive
Save energy
That's what I think.

Try and reduce your carbon footprint
Stop polluting the environment
Try to reuse the things that can be reused
Buy the green energy bulbs, they last longer
That's what I think.

Start recycling, it makes a difference
Try using the go green bags
If you are using paper remember to use both sides
Put your litter in the bin
That's what I think.

Remember to use wood instead of coal
Start eating the food you have grown
Don't pollute the air
Put used paper in the recycle bin
That's what I think.

Stop cutting down trees because we need them to breathe
Don't use your car a lot
Don't leave the lights on all night
That's what I think.

Remember to use things more than once
Don't throw your litter on the ground
Don't throw things away, use them again
Use renewable
That's what I think.

Samantha Gemmell (11)
Wellington School, Ayr

Reduce, Reuse, Recycle

R educe waste,
E nergy as well,
D usters work as well as Hoovers,
U se energy-efficient bulbs,
C an you help?
E verything should be used sparingly.

R euse paper,
E ach side is as clean as the next,
U se boxes and bags again and again,
S ome are made to be reused,
E verything could be reused if you try.

R ecycle as much as possible,
E very sheet of paper,
C heck if bottles can be recycled,
Y ou could recycle more than throw out,
C heck for recycling plants near you,
L et things be transformed into something new,
E ach and every one of them.

T he future should be preserved,
H elp to make a difference,
E ach and every one of you.

F ight for the future,
U se your potential,
T ry to make a difference,
U se less energy,
R educe, reuse, recycle,
E veryone listen to me!

Morven Archbold (10)
Wellington School, Ayr

Save Our Earth

Save our planet
Grow your food
Don't take the car
Only walk in a good mood
So come and join me, save the Earth.

I'm on a mission
To save your Earth
Switch off your light
Every night
So come and join me, save the Earth.

Don't drop litter from your street
Put it in the bin in the street
Use renewable energy
Don't kill the animals for fun
So come and join me, save the Earth.

Reduce the amount of paper you use
Remember to use both sides
Reuse the plastic green bags
To help save our environment
So come and join me, save the Earth.

So try to recycle
Would be nice
Get rid of pollution
It needs to stop
So come and join me, save the Earth.

Taylor Hollywood (11)
Wellington School, Ayr

Save Our Planet

Stop attacking trees,
Can't you hear them cry in pain?
Just to help one tree,
Use both sides of the paper,
So help save trees!

Give moths a break,
And turn off the lights.
Saving energy too,
It makes a lot of difference,
So turn off lights!

Animals run away,
From the frightening guns,
Game destroys the food chain,
So if a rabbit dies the fox starves,
So don't hunt for fun!

Dolphins die every year,
Because of pollution,
Fish get stuck in cans,
Oil destroys coral,
So stop polluting the sea!

Save the air,
Stop taking the car,
Take your bike,
Or maybe walk,
So we can help our planet!

Megan Bindoni (10)
Wellington School, Ayr

Help Save The World

Help me save the world
Recycle, reduce and even reuse
It's good for you
Homegrown food is the best
But not the food from the shops.

Help me save the world
Walk, cycle and even run
It's good for you
Don't use cars, they pollute
And even oil ruins the Earth.

Help me save the world
Reuse, save and even switch off
It's good for you
Energy-saving lights are the best
Not lights which you have to renew, as much!

Help me save the world
Help, help and even more help
It's good for you
The world needs your help
And so do I.

Help me save the world
Please, please and even more please
It's good for you
No pollution, much more energy
Hardly any money on your bills.

Charlotte Lochhead (11)
Wellington School, Ayr

127

Go Green!

Think about the energy that we use,
It's been all over the news.
We all use fuel and other things too,
There's lots of things that we do.
Go green, go green, go green!

Some people drop litter,
We just call them bitter.
Turn off the lights and turn off the tellys,
Go out on a walk and put on your wellies.
Go green, go green, go green!

Let's save the ocean,
Follow my motion.
Save the fish in the sea,
Come on and follow me.
Go green, go green, go green!

Don't go in the car,
Walk, it's not far.
Cycle or take the bus,
Come on, don't make a fuss.
Go green, go green, go green!

Don't shoot animals for fun,
Or all the animals will be done.
Don't cut down trees
And don't diss me.
Go green, go green, go green!

Rosalyn Thomson (11)
Wellington School, Ayr

Save The Planet

Save the world, it's going to die,
We have to help or pay a fine.
We have got to help,
Bring it back to life now!

Don't drop litter, don't drop gum,
It pays a lot for everyone else
To pick it up, clean it up
And get it off the high street.

Walk to school or cycle home,
Grow your food and have some fun.
It's not all bad and you'll
Have a great and wonderful time.

Don't shoot all the lovely animals
Or waste all our energy.
The oil is gone,
The coal is going and it won't last.

Reduce, reuse and recycle,
It isn't a lot to do to help.
Stop pollution, it won't hurt
And the trees will be saved.

The trees, the lovely, lovely trees,
The ocean, the lovely, lovely ocean.
The animals, the lovely, lovely animals,
The planet needs our lovely care.

Rachel Alner (10)
Wellington School, Ayr

Save The World

To save our world,
Grow your own food,
Use renewable energy
And save our environment,
Start to recycle and be happy,
Save the animals and don't hurt their feelings.

Reuse products every day
And save lots of energy,
Don't drop litter on the path,
Put it in the bin and feel good,
Don't take your car every day,
Walk with a grateful cheer.

Reduce paper as much as you can,
Instead of using another piece,
Turn to the other side,
Stop using coal for fires,
Instead use wood for it
And save the hemisphere.

This is a mission to save our world,
So to save it we have to do all these things
And it includes me and you,
And together we can make the Earth last and last,
At least for another thousand years,
So let's start to save the world.

Ryan Muir (12)
Wellington School, Ayr

Save Our Planet

Reduce, reuse, recycle.
Improve our world, walk to school.
Don't shoot animals, it's very cruel.
Stop pollution, it makes a mess.
Try to recycle, it's the best!
Now you know!

Reduce, reuse, recycle.
Save energy, switch off lights.
Grow your own food, it tastes nice.
Use renewable energy, it's the best!
Reduce your carbon footprint!

Reduce, reuse, recycle.
Reduce the amount of paper.
Why don't you use both sides?
That's how you reduce.
Give our planet a chance.
That's the name of the game!

Reduce, reuse, recycle.
Use a green bag.
It's made to be reused.
So why don't you use it for your goods?
That's the name of the game
So save our planet!

Liam Fitzsimmons (10)
Wellington School, Ayr

How Can I Make The World Better?

Driving along one day
How can I make the world a better place, Mum?
Don't worry we've done our bit, dump those bags over there
No Mum, we need to put them in the blue bin
That will make the world better!

Driving along one day
How can I make the world a better place, Mum?
Don't worry we've done our bit, smash those glasses against that wall
No Mum, we need to put them in the black bin
That will make the world better!

Driving along one day
How can I make the world a better place, Mum?
Don't worry we've done our bit, throw those dead flowers over there
No Mum, we need to put them in the brown bin
That will make the world better!

Driving along one day
How can I make the world a better place, Mum?
Well I think you know how
Yes Mum, I think I do
I have made the world a better place!

Harmen Lindsay (11)
Wellington School, Ayr

The Environment

The environment has issues,
Animals in fact or plants,
It has animals A to Z,
Every day lots die because of manmade materials,
The other percent, well figure it out for yourself.

Plants let out O_2
But what happens if someday plants get lots of CO_2 and can't recycle it?
All the plants will die and since there is no recycled O_2 we will die,
Plus if the flowers die the world won't be pretty,
It'll all be a dull world.

Insects help us,
They help us take away unwanted rubbish,
That means the world won't be full of rubbish,
The dung beetle helps take away dung,
So insects help us a lot.

All of these things help us,
The animals, the plants and even the insects,
But I'm missing something,
You,
You can help as well.

Jonathan Webb (11)
Wellington School, Ayr

Let's Make This World A Better Place

Wasps and bees
Trapped in the trees
Wolves and foxes
Stuck in boxes
Let's make this world a better place.

Carbon dioxide in the air
Chewing gum everywhere
Broken bottles lying around
Crisp packets on the ground
Let's make this world a better place.

Walking to school instead of driving
Or go on to the bus instead of skiving
The animals are extinct because of us
The animals just don't buzz because of us
Let's make this world a better place.

Why did the animals have to die?
No more rare species fly by
People just don't care
If we all did our bit
Then we wouldn't have a fit
We've made the world a better place.

Chloe Phillips (10)
Wellington School, Ayr

Our World

To save our world
Use less energy
Walk and cycle
Don't travel by car.

Switch off lights
In the night
Recycle what you can
Don't put it in the bin.

Reduce the amount of paper you use
Always use both sides
Grow your own food
Try and use less energy.

Stop pollution, it is everywhere
Cities and countries
Building to building
Streets and cities, it is everywhere.

To save our world
All you have to do
Is just use a bit less of everything
Just a bit, that's what you have to do.

Gregor Lynch (11)
Wellington School, Ayr

I'm On A Mission

I'm on a mission
To save the Earth
It needs to be greener
And a lot less meaner.

I'm on a mission
To get rid of pollution
It needs to stop
So get out the mop.

I'm on a mission
To get you to recycle
Use it twice
But more would be nice.

I'm on a mission
To make you greener
Try to walk to school
That would be really cool.

I'm on a mission
To save you
If you don't care
Then say goodbye to the polar bear!

Martin McHard (11)
Wellington School, Ayr

The World

Crisp packets flying around,
Broken glass lying on the ground,
Chewing gum stuck everywhere,
Carbon dioxide floating in the air,
Please, help me save the world!

Some old mattresses dumped in canals,
Plastic bags stuck in throats of animals,
Factories polluting the ozone layer,
People setting lots of snares,
Please, help me save the world!

Keep badgers digging at night,
Let the owls see you in their sight,
The rivers changing into seas,
Birds chattering,
Please, help me save the world!

So next time you eat a sweet,
Don't drop the wrapper at your feet,
Put it right in the bin,
Help to keep the world clean,
You would be helping save the world!

Sophie Kirk (11)
Wellington School, Ayr

What Would Happen?

What would happen if the world was covered in litter?
It might clog up and explode
Or shrink up into a prune.
It might dissolve into thin air.
That might be what would happen.

What would happen if the world was polluted?
It might be thickly covered in fog
Or we might have to wear gas masks.
It might become heavy and drop into space.
That might be what would happen.

What would happen if all the animals died?
We might be starving and thin and bony
Or we might die
And the world would shrivel like a dead leaf.
That might be what would happen.

So this is the tale of the world ending.
The people and animals would die.
Try to prevent this happening.
We could save the Earth.
That might be what would happen.

Amy Napier (11)
Wellington School, Ayr

Reduce, Reuse, Recycle

Chewing gum is such a pain.
We are stepping in it every day.
It is sticking to our shoes.
Chewing gum is getting in the way.
Reduce, reuse, recycle.

Wildlife is dying.
They are getting caught in our rubbish.
Fish are getting stuck in our plastic bags
And are suffocating.
Reduce, reuse, recycle.

Giant pandas are dying
Because of poachers.
The forests that they live in are being cut down.
They don't have very much food.
Reduce, reuse, recycle.

Use the recycling bins that your council have provided you with.
The blue one is for paper.
The black one is for bottles.
The green one is for your gardening waste.
Reduce, reuse, recycle.

Iona Hayes (11)
Wellington School, Ayr

The Planet Of Rubbish

There are lots of rubbish bags
And smoking ghastly fags.
There used to be wildlife
Now there's just no life.
This is the Planet of Rubbish.

You can definitely tell
That this is a rubbish hell.
Toxic gases in the air
Waste and rubbish everywhere.
This is the Planet of Rubbish.

Why oh why
Did creatures have to die?
But now it's been done
And there's simply no one.
This is the Planet of Rubbish.

If we all do our bit
Then we won't be like it.
Don't get in a mood
Because we all should.
This isn't the Planet of Rubbish.

Kenneth Manderson (11)
Wellington School, Ayr

Think!

Think how cool the world could be
If we all played our part!
Saving electricity and fuel,
Recycling everything possible,
More recycling, less landfills!

Think how cool the world could be
If we all played our part!
Looking after the wildlife,
Caring for our planet,
No more animals becoming extinct!

Think how cool the world could be
If we all played our part!
Polluting the atmosphere has got to stop,
Why should we do it?
We know it's wrong!

Think how cool the world could be
If we all played our part!
This world cannot survive without us,
So we need to make a start . . . *think!*

Yasmin Habib (11)
Wellington School, Ayr

Reduce, Reuse, Recycle

Reduce, reuse, recycle - that's the latest news,
Reduce the amount you use your car,
So that you can save the countryside,
And if you are lucky enough you may save a life.

Reduce, reuse, recycle - that's the latest news,
Reuse all of your plastic bags and your bottles too,
To stop landfills being created and spoiling our beautiful land,
So that our children can live here.

Reduce, reuse, recycle - that's the latest news,
Recycle your bottles and paper in the blue bin,
Your glass bottles and jars go into the black bin,
The brown bin is for weeds from the garden.

Reduce, reuse, recycle - that's the latest news,
Help to save our planet, that's what we have to do,
Stop the trees falling down and people shouting, 'Timber!'
Stop using up the Earth's valuable resources so that the Earth does not die.

Ivan Craig (11)
Wellington School, Ayr

Our World Today

Reduce, reuse, recycle
We need to save our world today
Before it disappears away
Do what you think is the best
Rely on other people to do the rest.

Reduce, reuse, recycle
Do you want to damage the air?
Do you want to damage the world beyond repair?
If you drive a car, go in a bus
Be like the rest of us.

Reduce, reuse, recycle
Put your rubbish in a bin
Paper, plastic, even tin
How would you like to have rubbish everywhere?
Don't be a litterbug and do your share.

Reduce, reuse, recycle
It will make the world a better place.

Kiera Hamilton (11)
Wellington School, Ayr

Save Your Home, Earth

Recycle, recycle, please recycle
Think of that landfill site, what a dirty mess
You should be ashamed of yourself, you're making the mess
Recycle, recycle, please recycle.

Animals, animals, poor animals
They're dying of waste dumped on the floor
Without them how will you live? How?
Animals, animals, poor animals.

Cars, cars, horrible cars
They breathe out dirty carbon, yuck
What can we do to help? Walk
Cars, cars, horrible cars.

You can help by recycling
Don't dump your litter on the floor
Help by walking, cycling or running
Save your home, Earth.

Zara Wardrop (11)
Wellington School, Ayr

Save The Environment

Recycle your rubbish, drink cans, paper,
Cardboard, wood, tin, bottles.
Why waste all this?
Save the environment.

Reuse plastic bags, paper, clothes
And other reusable things.
Why waste all this?
Save the environment.

Reduce your heating, carbon dioxide,
The amount of energy you use.
Why waste all this?
Save the environment.

So honestly, why waste all of this?
So reduce, reuse, recycle.
Thank you for saving the environment.
Save the environment.

Euan Cosh (10)
Wellington School, Ayr

Save The Environment

Recycle, reuse, grow your own food
Do all you can do to make the world good
Wasting the world is a crime on its own
So switch off the light or eat something homegrown
Save the environment.

The world is dying because of our mess
So people, save the world, do nothing less
Saving the world is the right thing to do
So come on people, I'm talking to you
Save the environment.

This land we live on is not the only one
In the ocean the rubbish weighs a tonne
So come on people, save the ocean
That's the only way to stop all the commotion
Save the environment.

Elspeth Jamieson (11)
Wellington School, Ayr

Improve The World

Don't cut down trees.
You'll hurt their leaves.
It's not cool to do it.
So just don't go through with it.
Leave them be and don't hurt any tree.

Don't drop litter, don't drop gum
And don't shoot animals with a gun.
Our bins aren't weighing a tonne.
Don't drop litter, put it in the bin.
Join the fight, you know it's right.

Don't take the car, don't take the bus.
Walk, don't make a fuss.
Turn off your tap or else do a lap.
Our Earth will soon turn into dust
And we will burst, so look after the Earth!

Shannon Cowan (11)
Wellington School, Ayr

146

Wild Beast

It headed towards me
With its red glowing eyes
I wondered what it could be
Fear rushed around inside me
I stood there, quiet and still
As it came in for the kill

It ran on four legs
Panting and growling
Gripping with its claws in the mud
Hungry for blood
As it came in for the kill

It lunged at me
Catching its claw upon my knee
I struck the ground hard
It climbed on me
Its foul breath in my face
As it came in for the kill

I take a closer look
It's licking my face
Its eyes are not red
No growling or howling
Not coming in for the kill

The feeling of fear vanishes
Not a wild beast
It is my dog.

Some people treat animals with no respect
Harming, starving, abandoning them
What do they see?
What do they think?
Are they afraid of a wild beast?

Lee Dyson (15)
Whiteheath Education Centre, Rowley Regis

The Street Mystery

Treading through the streets at night,
There's no one around,
Everyone's out of sight
'What was that? Who's there?'
Something running past really gives me a scare.

Rain pours down even faster now
I get soaked but I don't care how,
Walking further through the street
I see a shadow creep
I stop and wait,
Nothing. Too late.

But what was it on this cold wet day
Following me around like I was prey?
A cat? A dog? A relative? Friend?
Will I ever know?
I wonder when?

The world would be a better place
If everyone knew each other's face
No hiding around street bends
Waiting for someone to offend.

Amy Dyson (15)
Whiteheath Education Centre, Rowley Regis

Stop! Think!

Stop! Think! Don't cut trees down.
Think of the beauty and the majesty.
Think of the colours green and brown.
Think of the animals that call them home.

Sarah Gronow (14)
Whiteheath Education Centre, Rowley Regis

148

Conflict

Racism is very bad,
It really annoys me and makes me mad,
Why can't people just get along
Every day and sing a song?

War can stem from racial hate,
Everyone leaves and takes their mate,
Guns, bombs, tanks too,
Lots of shooting, work to do.

Hatred fills the soldiers there,
A lot worse than they could bear,
But in the end one side wins,
All the dead bodies put in the bin.

Poverty can be the output of war,
Not enough housing for the rich and poor,
Money, food, a shortage there is,
Still today in this world we live in.

Ashley Warner (15)
Whiteheath Education Centre, Rowley Regis

Poem On Litter

Litter . . .
All the litter on the floor,
It makes our world look so poor.

Orange cartons and crisp bags,
Tissue papers and cigarette fags.

We can also recycle,
It's easier than riding a bicycle.

It's easy to use a bin,
Just pop your litter right in!

Littering is polluting our environment,
So let's not litter, it's an easy assignment.

Tadala Kotamo
Whitton School, Twickenham

A Poem About Rainforest Animals Becoming Extinct

Insects and mammals,
But not camels,
They live in the rainforests,
They don't have names like Doris.

Hear the noise
Of a thousand animals,
Calling out for help.

High in the sky,
Or down beneath,
In every square inch,
You might feel a pinch.

Hear the noise
Of a thousand animals,
Calling out for help.

Hear the trees,
Crashing below,
Animals hold on
And might land in a pond.

Hear the noise
Of a thousand animals,
Calling out for help.

All types of animals,
Including cannibals,
Get cut with trees
And the bees.

Hear the noise
Of a thousand animals,
Calling out for help.

Killed for paper,
Which will be used later,
They didn't dance,
As they didn't have the chance.

Hear the noise,
Of a thousand animals,
Calling out for help.

Hannah Fern (12)
Whitton School, Twickenham

Stop War

War means death
War means destruction
War means fire
War means bombing
War means sorrow
War means turmoil
War means tears
War means guns
War means blood
War means confusion
War means explosions
War means mutilation
War means sickness
War means killing
War means occupation
War means loss

But after one side
Or the other side
Has finally had enough
And lays down their arms
To surrender and give up . . .

War means peace!

Jonathan Blakeley
Whitton School, Twickenham

To Make The World A Better Place

Bark from a tree nice and brown
Water from London town,
Green leaves and petals from a rose
Molten rock and camouflage clothes.

Help the monkeys or grow a tree
Then the whole world could see,
Let the light shine on your face
And let's make the world a better place.

Turn off your light by the wall
That would really help us all,
Earthworms from underground
Happy faces all around.

Help the monkeys or grow a tree
Then the whole world could see,
Let the light shine on your face
And let's make the world a better place.

In the Amazon there's no trees
So stop cutting them down, oh please, oh please
They give us oxygen all around
And suck up water from underground
This is a spell for everyone
After you mix it let's have fun, so

Help the monkeys or grow a tree
Then the whole world could see,
Let the light shine on your face
And let's make the world a better place!

Izzey Godfrey (12)
Whitton School, Twickenham

A Poem To Stop Droughts

River, river ever so dry
You can make some people cry
Come on river
You're making me quiver
Please river, why can't you grow?
You are not the raging river we know.

The river is flowing, flowing and growing,
The river is flowing down to the sea.

Please rain, come to us
Hurry, do not make a fuss
Please rain, please arrive
Come and make the water levels rise
Come on rain
Come and rain on the dusty plain.

The river is flowing, flowing and growing,
The river is flowing down to the sea.

Come on rain, we need you here
We need to see you nice and clear
Please river, please flow
We need you to make the crops grow
Here you are at last
Quickly now, make the river flow very fast.

The river is flowing, flowing and growing,
The river is flowing down to the sea.

Tom Cope (12)
Whitton School, Twickenham

Global Warming Disappear

An exhaust from a car
That has not travelled far
A cow's fart
And an aeroplane part.

Stir it up on the grass
Don't let anyone pass.

Add the roots of a tree
And the water from the sea
Add a load of ice
And it's the start of something nice.

Stir it up on the grass
Don't let anyone pass.

Go ahead and add a bike
Then a T-shirt made by Nike
Leave it overnight
Then add a tarantula bite.

Stir it up on the grass
Don't let anyone pass.

Now potion, sink and cure the Earth
And make it a brand new birth.

Lewis Turner
Whitton School, Twickenham

Racism Poem

People are black and white,
Don't mean you need to fight.

Everyone's a different race,
So be proud of your face.

Don't worry what people say
And just enjoy your day!

Kimberley Scott (13)
Whitton School, Twickenham

Environmental Poem

Here is an environmental poem
That you're about to read.
If we all work together
We can all do a good deed.

Even though you must keep your teeth clean,
Please make sure you
Turn the tap off in-between.

Saving water from going down your sink,
Will give those people in the Third World a refreshing drink,
Driving in your car is a different matter.

Get on your bike
Be fit and not get fatter.
However if it rains
Use one of London's many buses or trains.

Last but not least,
If we work together to keep this world greener,
Do not litter,
But recycle your rubbish
To keep the world cleaner.

Adele Wreford
Whitton School, Twickenham

Greener Way

For the Big Green Poetry Machine,
Trying to make the world so green;
Lots of litter not put in the bin,
With bags, pots and silver tins,
Wasting lots of electricity,
Now there won't be enough for you and me,
All the green being polluted,
Right here in London, it's just not suited;
Making this planet a greener place
So it won't be getting on people's cases.

Bradley Wilson (13)
Whitton School, Twickenham

Spell To Make The World A Greener Place

The green from the leaves
The bark from the trees
In go the creatures
The birds and the bees
Burning bright, the mixture gleams
More and more, the world will be green
Get all the litter
Off the street
The cartons and cans
From the stuff that we eat
Burning bright, the mixture gleams
More and more, the world will be green
Put in the heat
From the sun
Put on the lid
And now we're done!

Robert Cummings
Whitton School, Twickenham

Spell Of Poaching

All the poaching has to stop
Now make all their weapons drop.

Tail of wolf and rhino's horn
No more fur coats shall be worn.

Cheetah's teeth and claws of bear
Elephant's tusk and fur of hare.

Dolphin nets and blood of whales
We're so sick of horrible tales.

Fangs of snakes and crocodiles' skins
No more soup made with sharks' fins.

All the poaching has to stop
Now make all their weapons drop.

Jens Formesyn (12)
Whitton School, Twickenham

156

Pollution

Please don't litter, it causes pollution,
Make it your New Year's resolution,
Don't throw your litter away in haste,
Recycle instead, it makes less waste,
In the big green bin it goes,
Recycled, reused and no one knows,
When you drive, it makes you pollute,
Walk to work, when you commute,
Chemicals and fumes fill the air,
Don't pollute if you really care,
In the big green bin it goes,
Recycled, reused and no one knows,
Plastic bags ruin our Earth,
Think instead, what's it worth?
We need to stop all the pollution,
Don't pollute, it's not the solution!

Daniel Kemp (12)
Whitton School, Twickenham

Help Save The Earth

It doesn't hurt to help the Earth,
It's been slowly dying since its birth.
Recycle plastic, paper and glass,
This helps the Earth to last.
Short distances you can walk,
Grow a new plant with a different stalk.
Help reduce the carbon gases,
The air will be clearer by the masses.
Help reduce the gas CO_2
The world will be better for me and you.

Charlotte O'Driscoll (12)
Whitton School, Twickenham

If We All Stayed Green

In the recycling bin
Goes paper and card
And no!
It doesn't have to be too hard
Not forgetting the bottles and cans
Which also could be made into fans.

The world will be really clean
If we all just stayed green.

It's against the law
To drop litter on the floor
That's why we have bins
To drop our litter right in.

Now the world is really clean
Because we have all turned green.

Zowe Kotamo (12)
Whitton School, Twickenham

Young Writers
Information

We hope you have enjoyed reading this book - and that
you will continue to enjoy it in the coming years.

If you like reading and writing poetry drop us a line, or
give us a call, and we'll send you a free information pack.

Alternatively if you would like to order further copies of
this book or any of our other titles, then please give us a
call or log onto our website at www.youngwriters.co.uk

Young Writers Information
Remus House
Coltsfoot Drive
Peterborough
PE2 9JX
(01733) 890066